# FOODS
## *for* Health
## & Healing

## REMEDIES & RECIPES

Based on the teachings of

## Yogi Bhajan, PhD

D0482889

*Foods for Health and Healing* is a guide to ancient remedies which have been used over the years. *They are not proven cures.* They should be employed judiciously and, in the case of mono diets or prolonged fasts, with competent medical supervision. In the case of serious illness, a doctor should be consulted.

Edited by Gurubanda Singh Khalsa & Parmatma Singh Khalsa
For the Kundalini Research Institute.
Based on Material compiled by Siri Amir Singh Khalsa, D.C.
From the teachings of Yogi Bhajan
Cover art and illustration by Siri Gian Kaur Khalsa
Editorial Assistant - Dharm Darshan Kaur Khalsa
Back cover photo by Satsimran Kaur
Printed in Michigan by Sheridan Books

The editors wish to express their deep appreciation for the selfless service of the many friends, family members, and health professionals who tested recipes. Special thanks to Jaswant Singh Khalsa, M.D., for his contributions to Chapters Two and Four, Guru Siri Kaur Khalsa and Tarn Taran Kaur Khalsa for their help with Chapter Eight, Cindra Joy Khalsa for her recipe for *Chiles and Cheese*, and Siri Ved Kaur Khalsa for permission to reprint recipes from her book, *Conscious Cookery*.

©1983 by Kundalini Research Institute. All rights reserved, including the right to reproduce this book or portions thereof in any form, except for the inclusion of brief quotations in review.

*Published by*
*Kundalini Research Institute*

ISBN 978-0-913852-15-6

# CONTENTS

# LIST OF RECIPES

*Editors' Note:*

# About Yogi Bhajan

We are very privileged to present Yogi Bhajan's teachings on food and healing. When he arrived in America in 1969, Yogi Bhajan brought with him a wealth of ancient knowledge on a wide array of subjects — yoga, meditation, healing, massage, Indian cuisine and male-female relationships, as well as astrology, numerology and herbology. It has been his express purpose to transmit this knowledge and preserve it in the West. This volume is a small step toward the fulfillment of that goal.

Yogi Bhajan was raised in the Punjab, in an area which is now in Pakistan. As he was an exceptional child, his parents arranged for him to study with several leading teachers of yoga, meditation and religious studies. He mastered Kundalini Yoga at an early age, and then went on to study White Tantric Yoga, in which men and women meditate together under the guidance of a master to cleanse their subconscious minds. He graduated college with a degree in economics and went on to take a post in the Indian government. Maintaining his inner discipline as a yogi, he lived the life of a householder, marrying and raising three children. In his thirty-ninth year, he left India for America where he began teaching Kundalini Yoga, White Tantric Yoga, and conscious vegetarian living.

1

Yogi Bhajan established the 3HO (Healthy, Happy, Holy) Foundation which offers classes in yoga, meditation and vegetarian diet in over a hundred cities throughout the world. A devout Sikh, he is the religious leader of the Sikh religion in the West. He has been a pioneer n bringing together the leaders of diverse religions in order to further the causes of world peace and mutual understanding. He received his doctorate for original research in the field of human communication.

Yogi Bhajan brings a unique blend of knowledge and experience to the subject of food and health. The son of a medical doctor, he would often travel with his father to visit patients. At his father's side, he learned that a doctor must be aware of the whole patient - his body, mind and spirit. - before prescribing treatment. During his years of government service, he was well known in India as a yogi and a healer, and was often called upon to treat people who had found no help through other means. Using a combination of diet and herbal therapy, yoga therapy, massage and skeletal adjustment, he put into practice the knowledge he had gleaned in his early years. Since coming to America, has has applied these techniques in treating the ailments most common to this part of the world, developing his own therapies for drug abuse, nicotine addiction, alcoholism, stress, "burn-out" and even "smog fatigue." He has inspired the creation of a network of holistic healing clinics throughout North America, in which ancient and modern medical techniques are combined to bring about lasting positive changes in a person's health. His teachings on food and health were also the impetus for the establishment of a chain of Golden Temple restaurants and food stores, and for the publication of the *Golden Temple Vegetarian Cookbook*.

Yogi Bhajan teaches regularly in Los Angeles and New Mexico while maintaining a schedule of courses and workshops in cities throughout America and Europe. Anyone who has attended his classes knows that they are a unique blend of anecdotes and fables, humor and profundity, with metaphysics, music and meditations. He has a free-wheeling style which spans all times

2

and places, from the dialogues of Krishna and Arjuna to the crises and challenges of today's world. While the topics of his classes are many and varied, each class transmits to the students an experience of heightened awareness.

Since Yogi Bhajan spends most of his time traveling and teaching (rather than writing books), we have compiled this book from information in his lectures of the first fourteen years. This book is intended primarily for the layperson or the beginning student of the healing arts. As such, there are certain remedies, therapies and diagnostic aids which are not within its scope. For those who would like to delve deeper into the spoken words of Yogi Bhajan, Kundalini Yoga products, as well as Yogi Tea, spiritual music, herbal supplements, and body care products are also available from Ancient Healing Ways, Inc. and their website: *www.a-healing.com* (Listed on page 133).

# How to Use This Book

This book is more than a directory of remedies and recipes for health. It is a guide for conscious living through the selection and preparation of simple, delicious, nourishing foods.

It is divided into several sections. Chapters Two through Four contain useful guidelines for selecting, preparing, serving and digesting the food you eat. The suggestions in these chapters can help you to form heathful habits of eating. Chapter Five contains information about common vegetarian foods and their healing properties. Through reading it, you may gain a greater appreciation of these delicious "gifts of the earth," and may find some foods which seem particularly suited to your needs. Chapters Six through Eight describe specific foods and health recommendations for men, women and children. Each of these groups has certain special food requirements. Chapter Nine talks briefly about fasting, and how to safely and intelligently use fasting and mono diets to cleanse your body and guard against disease. Chapter Ten is a directory of body systems and their common ailments. You can use this section to learn about foods, diets and other recommendations which can help you to strengthen your body and to overcome any weaknesses.

There is some unavoidable duplication of information between Chapter Five, "Foods for Health and Healing," and Chapter Ten. Of the two, Chapter Ten is the more complete as far as treatments for various ailments are concerned. If there is a particular ailment or condition which interests you, or a particular food about which you would like to learn more, use the Index.

Following Chapter Ten is a section of healing recipes, listed in alphabetical order. References to these recipes appear throughout the text, printed in italics for easy recognition. At the back of the book, you'll find several useful guides: "Sources of Special Foods" — where to find various unusual or imported foods; "3HO Healing Network" — a partial listing of holistic health practitioners who employ some of the teachings contained in this book in their medical or healing practices, as well yoga centers that specialize in Kundalini Yoga therapy; and finally, a list of "Books on Related Topics" by Yogi Bhajan and others which you might like to read if you find sections of this book especially interesting.

# Chapter One:

# Food as Medicine

We live in an age of many diseases and many forms of ill health. For each malady that plagues modern man, there are a host of potential remedies and cures. Modern medicine offers us surgery, radiation therapy, chemotherapy and a staggering array of pharmaceuticals. For those who would choose less orthodox routes, there are chiropractic, acupuncture, homeopathy, nutritional therapy, and a long list of alternative methods of healing, both new and old. Each of them is useful in its own way.

In ancient times, before the development of modern science, people had fewer alternatives when it came to taking care of their health. In their simple wisdom, they looked upon the food they ate as the source of their continued good health and as the cure for what ailed them. Food was their medicine. They learned the principles of healthful eating, and they discovered the hidden properties of common foods and herbs which could purify their bodies, correct imbalances which were the sources of disease, and even heal damaged tissue.

In time, people learned to make medicines from the extracts of healing foods and herbs. Many of them are still used in India and in other countries where preindustrial culture still survives. They heal more slowly than modern medicines but they are nearly free of side effects. When man finally learned the science of chemistry, he synthesized chemical substitutes for the natural medicines he had previously used. Now, the vast majority of our modern medicines are manufactured without any relationship to the natural remedies of the past. They are often amazingly effective in masking or eliminating the symptoms of disease, but they may fail to deal with the underlying causes of disease, and may produce side effects which are as bad as or worse than the disease itself.

Today it appears that we have come full circle. People are once again trying to understand the basics of healthful living. Our emphasis has shifted to preventive medicine, and there is renewed interest in the simpler methods of the past. At this time, it would be worthwhile to look again at the most basic key to our continuing good health: the food we eat.

# Chapter Two:

# Choosing Your Foods

Our lives have many facets: how we think, how we behave, how we project, how we communicate — but the one facet of our lives which forms a base for all the others is how we eat. For most of us this is not a matter of conscious training but of haphazard experience. We eat according to our childhood experiences; according to what looks good, smells good or tastes good; according to our whims, our appetites, our emotions or our circumstances; even according to our social status. Really, we should be eating to fulfill the needs of our bodies, minds and spirits. You've heard the saying, "You are what you eat." Each time you eat food, you create your future self.

## NUTRITIOUS AND SUSTAINING FOODS

How, then, do we know which foods are best for us? First, let us consider two ways of looking at the value of foods. Foods can be *nutritious* and they can also be *sustaining*. Nutritious foods are those which give your body the fuel it needs to function. Nutritious foods give you energy and strength. Although this is not primarily a text on nutrition, you should choose your foods with their nutritive values in mind. Generally speaking, whole, fresh and natural foods possess nutrients that are more easily assimilated by your body than their canned, frozen or processed equivalents.

Sustaining foods are those that heal your body and keep it well. The sustaining value of a food is based on a combination of its nutritional content, its texture, its taste, its aroma, the way it is prepared, and its specific effect on the body. Often, a combination of foods prepared together has a sustaining value which is far more potent than the sum of the ingredients. This book is primarily about sustaining foods. If your diet consists of foods which are both nutritious and sustaining, and you are careful to eat only what you can digest, then you have laid the groundwork for a healthy and happy life.

## SUN FOODS, GROUND FOODS, AND EARTH FOODS

A useful way of choosing the foods you eat is according to the environments in which they grow. *Sun foods* are those which grow more than three feet above the ground. Clinging to trees or vines, they absorb the maximum energy from the sun and the least from the earth. For this reason, they are considered to be very high, etheric foods. If you want to elevate your consciousness beyond the affairs of this earth, then a diet of sun fruits and nuts, perhaps with a little milk, would be recommended. In India, this is the most common diet of yogis, saints and holy men. Because these foods have a quickening, lightening effect on the body and the nervous system, sun foods are especially suitable for people with large-boned body types and sluggish nervous energy. Elderly people should also include a larger portion of these foods in their diets since they are easy on the digestive system and are very stimulating to the higher centers of the brain. Generally speaking, one's diet should include a greater proportion of sun foods during the summer or in warm climates.

*Ground foods* grow within three feet above the ground. They absorb less energy from the sun than sun foods and more from the earth. As such, they are high in nutrients and have great cleansing value. Normally, the heart of a nutritious and sustaining diet is made up of ground foods like beans, rice, breads and green vegetables. Many of our most basic cleansing diets, like steamed greens or *Mung Beans and Rice,* are also from this group.

9

*Earth foods* are those which grow below the ground. They absorb great energy from the earth, but they only absorb sun energy indirectly. Foods from this group, like onions, garlic and ginger, are primarily used for their healing properties. Also, since these foods grow closest to the earth, they can give you great energy when you have a lot of worldly business or hard work to accomplish. *Beet-Carrot Casserole* and *Potent Potatoes* are examples of the highly energizing food in this group. Because these foods are so rich in "earth energy," they are often prescribed for people who are relatively deficient in this type of energy. Typically, these are small-boned people, people with tall, thin frames, and those with nervous or agitated dispositions. The proportion of earth foods in our diets should normally be increased in the winter and in colder climates.

## SATTVA, TAMAS AND RAJAS

Ancient Indian theory divides all matter, including human beings and their foods, into three broad categories or states of being, *sattva, rajas* and *tamas*. Sattvas means pure essence. It represents the etheric quality, the purely meditative mind. Rajas refers to the energy which gets things done, which seeks to accomplish, achieve or create. It is the quality of worldly power and the sexual drive. Tamas is the regressive property of inertia and decay. In human beings, it refers to the qualities of gluttony, indulgence and sloth.

Each of these three properties is associated with types of foods. Sattvic foods include most of the fruit and vegetable kingdoms, especially sun foods and ground foods. Rajasic foods include the stimulating herbs and spices. Many of the earth foods fall into this group. Tamasic foods include all forms of meat, fish, poultry and eggs, as well as alcohol and intoxicating drugs.

Since you create your future self with every bite, you can easily judge which types of foods are most appropriate to your aims. For people who are free to live a quiet, contemplative life, a strict diet of sattvic food is perfect. For people who wish to maintain a meditative mind, but who also must live and work in the "real world," a diet consisting primarily of sattvic foods with some rajasic foods is best. For those who practice heavy disciplines which transmute sexual energy into spiritual energy, like Kundalini Yoga or some of the martial arts, a certain amount of rajasic food in the diet is required. Tamasic food is best avoided.

## RAW AND COOKED FOOD

Many books have been written about the advantages of eating raw foods. Their authors correctly state that most foods lose a certain amount of their vitamins and minerals when they're cooked. They also point to the beneficial effect that eating lots of roughage has upon the action of the intestines. Some people, however, have gone so far as to suggest that only raw foods

*11*

should be eaten. Although this may be useful periodically for cleansing purposes or for survival training, a more sensible approach is a healthy balance between raw and cooked foods in the diet.

Some of the minerals and metals in vegetables, though plentiful in the raw form, are locked into large molecules so that they are unavailable for our nourishment unless cooked. Cooking is a kind of chemistry. Many of the healing foods described in this book derive their therapeutic qualities through the blending of their ingredients in the cooking process. Simply eating the ingredients raw would not achieve the same results. Neither would they produce a very tasty and attractive meal. As we shall see, the taste and the appearance of food contribute importantly to its sustaining value.

## THE VARIETIES OF TASTE

The Indian word for taste is *rasa,* and there is an entire science built around the uses and combinations of tastes. Taste is not seen merely as a pleasant or unpleasant attribute of food, but as an important factor affecting our health and disposition. It is similar to color therapy. Researchers have found that colors can affect our mental and emotional states, even causing or healing physical disorders. Like the primary colors, there are six primary tastes: sweet, sour, salty, pungent, bitter and astringent. Each has a different effect and should be balanced in the normal diet.

Sweet tastes are strengthening, pleasing and nourishing to the body. In excess, however, they can cause mucus, lassitude, indigestion, frequent colds and obesity.

Sour tastes stimulate the appetite and digestive secretions, excite the mind, and strengthen the energy flow to the organs. In excess, they can contribute to fevers, inflammations, burning sensations, looseness in the body, and impurities of the blood.

Salty tastes dilute mucus, increase the appetite, and aid in digestion. Too much salty food may cause debility, excess fluid, impotency, wrinkling of the skin, hyperacidity and inflammation.

Pungent tastes aid in the assimilation of food, excite the organs, dry up excess fluids, heal ulcers, soothe itching, remove lassitude and combat obesity. Used imprudently, they can destroy semen and cause fatigue, giddiness, loss of strength, thirst and pain in the body.

The bitter taste appetizes, clears the throat, sharpens the intellect, and is beneficial to the skin and flesh. In excess, it may give rise to headaches and loss of strength.

The astringent taste is soothing and cooling. It decreases mucus and acts as a blood purifier. When used in excess it may cause flatulence, constipation, pains in the chest, emaciation and thirst.

Learning to blend the six tastes healthfully and effectively in a balanced diet is an art which is perfected through observation and experience. We've given you "a taste" of the science of tastes so that you can more fully appreciate its importance.

## ACIDIFYING AND ALKALINIZING FOODS

Another factor to consider in choosing your food is how it affects the acid-alkaline balance of your body once it is digested. The yogic tradition states that for maximum health and mental balance the blood should be slightly alkaline. When the blood becomes relatively acidic, then a pathological condition results. The body becomes more vulnerable to serious illness, chronic ailments and premature aging.

Our metabolism, our enzyme activity, our respiration and circulation are all profoundly affected by shifts in our blood pH (the scientific measure of acidity/alkalinity). These shifts do not happen suddenly, as the result of a single meal, but over a long period of time, as a result of our overall diet. A healthy person can thus make his blood more alkaline by changing his diet. Sweet and sour fruits, green vegetables, legumes, milk, yogurt, *paneer,* cottage cheese and buttermilk are all excellent alkalinizers. Some of these foods, like citrus fruits, are acidic in their natural states but have an alkalinizing effect on the blood. Alkalinizing food rebuilds and tones organs, nerves and glands. It helps maintain good health, and keeps one balanced, calm and reflective.

Meat, fish, eggs and most starches (including sweets) acidify the blood. Fats like *ghee,* butter, margarine, and oil are neutral foods, but they are also highly concentrated, and therefore, hard to digest. Eating them in excess can also have an acidifying effect, since the body produces a surplus of acid in an attempt to digest them. Too much concentrated food taxes the digestive system and weakens related organs like the pancreas, gall bladder and liver. These effects are even more pronounced in children under twelve because their immature organs are even less capable of dealing with these heavy foods.

A good balance of acid and alkaline-producing foods in your diet is about two-thirds alkaline and one-third acid. (The average American diet is almost exactly the reverse.) So make vegetables the heart of your diet, along with fruits, nuts, legumes, and simple dairy products. Cut down on sweets, starchy foods and protein, and be moderate in your use of fats and oils. You'll feel better.

## WHAT ABOUT PROTEIN?

Most Americans have a protein fixation. They feel that they cannot live and their children's health will be in danger if they do not consume huge quantities of protein. This is especially true of men who feel that their physical and sexual power is dependent upon their daily intake of protein, particularly meat. As we shall see, almost the exact opposite is true. Women have been sold on the protein kick as a means of losing weight. "High protein diets," in which eighty percent of the diet is protein, including meat, fish and eggs, continue to be popular. Why? Much of the credit must go to the meat lobby in this country, which has convinced the American people that they need to consume more animal flesh per person than almost any other society on earth.

Actually, the body does not require a great deal of protein. (The World Health Organization has determined that the average adult requires thirty-five to forty grams of protein per day. The average American consumes one hundred twenty grams!) As long as you include some simple dairy products and eat a wide array of vegetables, especially greens, you should not really be concerned about it. The problem is that of all the food groups, protein is the hardest to digest. Too much protein leads to what we call "protein poisoning," and it will kill you — slowly. Excess protein in the digestive tract makes the liver and related glands overwork to the point that they may be permanently weakened. The excess toxins released into the system can cause body odor as well. Visitors from poorer vegetarian countries often complain that Americans have a very strong smell!

Although eating too much protein is, in itself, a problem, a much bigger problem is eating meat. We'll not consider the moral implications of eating meat. Strictly from a health point of view, eating meat is unwise, and that includes eggs. Eggs, like other meats, are a concentrated animal protein. Why is animal protein bad? When an animal dies, its proteins coagulate within a few hours. They undergo a process called "autoputrefaction" in which the original substance begins to break down and decay, releasing various toxins. When you eat meat, it cannot be completely broken down in the upper digestive tract, and so the process of decay and release of toxins continues in the colon. These toxins can initially be absorbed by the liver, but eventually even the liver can't handle them and they pollute the body. Vegetable proteins, by comparison, do not undergo autoputrefaction (unless they are rotten before they are eaten). Their main residue is cellulose, which is completely inert.

There are other reasons for not eating meat as well. We have already seen that meat is among the most acid-producing foods, and that eating meat as the main element in your diet will lead to acidic blood. Acidic blood is an ideal environment for the development of cancer. Studies linking meat diets with breast cancer bear this out. Meat is also among the greatest sources of cholesterol, which contributes to heart disease, hardening of the arteries and senility. Most animals which are raised for their meat today are fed a variety of chemicals and hormones to make them grow faster and bigger. You wouldn't take hormones without a doctor's orders, but you do ingest them in small quantities when you eat most commercially-produced meats.

Many diseases which commonly occur in this country are relatively rare in countries where little meat is eaten. In a place like southern India, where almost everyone eats a simple diet of rice, lentils and yogurt, you will find very little cancer, heart disease, and impotency. True, people are very poor, and you will find problems of malnutrition, infant mortality, and contagious diseases, but the diseases which now so plague the West are almost entirely absent. Should we close our eyes to the facts?

Current trends seem to suggest that people in the West are beginning to revise their eating habits. For a long time, Americans felt that they had to have the biggest cars with the biggest engines which burned the most gas. . . . Now they are beginning to learn that economy and efficiency are virtues as well. A smaller car with a highly efficient engine can go just as fast and be just as much fun to drive. Perhaps this thinking will carry over to food as well. Americans have long believed that more protein, bigger beefsteaks, and more food were the way to a strong and healthy body. Perhaps they will come to recognize that lighter, more nourishing food, in smaller quantities, will build a body that runs more efficiently, requires less costly maintenance, and lasts longer, without the need of a surgical overhaul. The lion is a great meat eater, and he is called the king of the jungle, but no animal can match the elephant, a complete vegetarian, for pure strength.

# Chapter Three:

# Preparing, Serving & Enjoying Your Food

In recent years, people have become increasingly aware of basic nutrition. We count calories, worry about getting enough protein, avoid cholesterol or watch out for iron deficiency. But only a fool would argue that the experience of eating food is simply the assimilation of various nutrients. It has often been theorized that science will someday develop a super-pill containing all the nourishment our bodies require so that we need never stop for meals again. Not only would life lose one of its great joys, but we would become considerably less healthy in the bargain. The conscious preparation, serving and enjoyment of food adds to our lives (and to our health) in more ways than one.

Let's reflect upon the experience of eating. Surely each of us knows what it's like to have finished a tasty meal, well prepared, taken in a leisurely fashion in the company of friends. As you set down your napkin and slide your chair back from the table, you feel a deep relaxation come over you, a sort of cozy and drowsy feeling. You naturally want to sit and relax for a while, perhaps even doze. Who can put a price on such a thoroughly enjoyable meal? It provides a necessary break for our bodies and minds from the routine of the day. It does wonders to relieve the disease-producing stress of our lives.

Then again, there is the busy man who, buried behind his newspaper, gulps down the last few bites of his food, and when asked, "How was your lunch?" must stop and ponder for a moment, "What did I eat?"

Certainly there are times when, despite our best efforts to plan, we feel forced to take a bite on the run, simply to give our bodies enough fuel to keep going. Nonetheless, the first general rule of healthful eating is *take the time to eat consciously*. If you can't, then don't eat at all.

A second, related rule is, *eat only in a pleasant, relaxing environment*. Any restauranteur knows that only half the key to success is serving delicious food; the other half is creating a desirable atmosphere. Soft lighting, attractive decor, pleasant service — we go to restaurants as much for these features as we do for good food. In fact, it may be said that we go to *restaurants* to *rest,* to feel relaxed enough that we can really enjoy and digest our food. In our homes, we can create relaxing environments by spending a few extra minutes to set the table nicely, by eliminating distractions like TV and radio which draw our attention away from our food, and by practicing good manners. Treat yourself and your family as if you deserve the best, imagine that each meal is a most special affair, and no matter how simple the menu or how humble your surroundings, your meals will give you health, security and sustenance which money can't buy.

That brings us to our next point. *Your food should be served gracefully.* When your food is placed before you, just the appearance of it should send a signal to your brain: this food is going to delight me and nourish me and I'm going to feel good! Then you immediately relax, your digestive juices start flowing and you feel very loved. Even if it is the most nutritious food, prepared from the freshest ingredients by the best gourmet cook, if it is simply thrown on the plate and served with a begrudging or hostile attitude, you might as well be eating cardboard. It will not take care of your body.

Serving your food gracefully is particularly important if you live alone and must serve yourself. Many people in this situation do themselves a great injustice by not taking the time to prepare decent meals. In the name of convenience, they come to depend upon fast foods, or worse yet, they stand in front of the open refrigerator and have an impromptu "meal" without even closing the door! Even if your dinner is just a single boiled potato, you can still place it in a shallow bowl, cut it in half, add a little butter, perhaps even a sprig of parsley, set it on the table before you, and enjoy. It will do more for your mind and body than ten bags of fries at the local burger stop.

After your food has been gracefully set before you, *take a minute to reflect upon your gratitude for the gift of food.* Every religion in the world has some sort of prayer that is said before eating. Why? Because it fulfills a natural balance in the universe. We have been provided with sustenance, therefore we must, in some way, acknowledge the Source of that sustenance. Even if you are a totally unreligious person who has no concept of God or a supreme power, you can still feel grateful to life, or to the universe, or to "mother earth" — however you choose to think about it — for the gift of your continuing existence.

*Prepare your food with love and care.* We often hear people say, "This meal was prepared with lots of love." What we may not realize is that it's true. Our thoughts and our feelings do go into the food we prepare. Science is slowly beginning to discover that our thoughts affect the world around us and the people around us just as much as our actions do. Yogis take this for granted. They say that if you want to conquer the world, first conquer your own mind. Learn to project only positive thoughts and the entire world will reflect positively upon you. If you want to learn to heal with foods, then think positive, healing thoughts while you are preparing it. Your food will have all its nutritive and sustaining value, plus the healing power of your thoughts.

There is a beautiful story from India which illustrates this point. Once there was a childless couple who wanted very much to have a son. They prayed to Lord Shiva, one of the Hindu deities, and finally their wish was granted. But there was one condition: Their son would not live beyond his twenty-fifth birthday. Nonetheless, the couple was very happy. Their son grew up to be healthy, well-mannered and intelligent, and soon it became time for him to

*19*

be married. His father went to considerable lengths to find a suitable bride. Finally, he found the daughter of a very devotional family and, feeling quite satisfied, made all the arrangements for the wedding. At first, the young man's mother objected that it would be wrong to marry him to a woman who would be widowed so soon, but his father insisted that there would be no sorrow in this couple's life. Everything would work out fine.

The young people were married and the years passed. As the young man approached his twenty-fifth birthday, his mother became filled with fear and sadness, but the father somehow remained calm, assuring his wife that nothing bad would happen. The dreaded day came and went without incident. And then the next day, and the next. The young man's mother was relieved but perplexed. How could it be? Lord Shiva himself had fixed the date. The father, seeing that his wife was deeply disturbed by this turn of events, suggested that she come along with him to their son's house, where she would find the answer to her unspoken question.

They arrived before dawn and stationed themselves outside a window where, in the dim light of the small kitchen, they could see their young daughter-in-law preparing breakfast for their son. They watched as she churned the fresh milk into butter, and with every rotation of the churn she chanted, "Shiva." Then she placed the butter in a pan on the stove to make ghee, and as she stirred the melting butter, she sang, "Shiva, Shiva." Likewise, as she chopped the fresh onions and garlic, the name of her heavenly Master was on her lips. And as she folded the spices into the soft dough of the *parantha,* her clear, sweet voice chanted longingly, "Shiva, Shiva, Shiva."

After a while, the simple meal over which she had labored for several hours was served to her husband. He ate it with great relish and then headed off to work. As the old couple headed home, the woman said to the man, "It was nice to see our daughter-in-law serving her husband with such devotion, but I still don't understand how it is that he is still alive." He explained,

"My dear, it is true that Lord Shiva decreed that our son's life was to be limited, but even Lord Shiva must heed the prayers of his devotees. You saw the way that woman prayed to Lord Shiva as she fixed the food. Her prayers went right into the food itself. Each day, death is waiting to grab our son, and each day he eats that food and death has to stay away. As long as they keep up this divine routine, our son cannot die."

That is why very religious people make it a practice to chant or pray constantly while preparing food. They want their minds to reflect only upon the Creator so that the entire creativity of the universe may be delivered through their food. Whatever your religious beliefs may be, assess your own consciousness before preparing a meal. Are your thoughts or feelings the kind which you would *like to eat,* or which you would want others to eat? Then, in whatever way you know how, clear your mind and fill it with thoughts of health and good wishes for all who will partake of the food you prepare.

# Chapter Four:

# Digesting &
# Eliminating Your Food

Equally as important as what you eat and how you eat is whether or not you can digest and eliminate the food you eat. Our systems are designed to extract the life-giving, nourishing elements in food and then efficiently dispose of the waste. If we cannot properly digest the food we eat, then our bodies will not be properly nourished. If we cannot eliminate the waste products within a short period of time, then our bodies will be poisoned by what we have failed to eliminate.

This chapter contains ten guidelines for healthful digestion and elimination of food. Following them may not seem easy, but it is my obligation to share them with you. As is the case with most good habits, once they are ingrained in your daily routine, they can be followed almost effortlessly, and you will be the happier and healthier for it. For those who have chronic problems with digestion or elimination, following these guidelines may be of some help in restoring their systems to normalcy. *For more information on correcting chronic disorders, see Chapter Ten.* If the problem is severe, consult your physician.

*1. Eat to live, don't live to eat.* We who live on this planet have been blessed with a wonderful variety of delicious and nourishing foods to eat. How lucky we are that the substances needed to give us life can provide such enjoyment as well. The problem is that for some people food becomes such a distraction and such a heavy source of gratification that it can really be said that they "live to eat." If you are constantly nagged by the desire to eat, then you can never consciously eat for health. You will eat too much and you will eat the wrong things at the wrong times because you cannot help yourself.

For some people, the constant desire for food may be a physiological problem. For others, it may be deeply psychological. But for most of us, it is simply a case of poor habits resulting in a lack of discipline. Our minds are not properly trained, so that when we are bored, upset, tired or distracted, we allow the thought of eating food to fill the gap. The answer is simple: Become more disciplined. When you feel the urge to eat and it is not your regular meal time, ask yourself, "Does my body really require more food at this time, or do I have some other reason for wanting to eat?" If your reason is of the "other" variety, be strong and don't eat. It may seem hard at first, but it will get easier.

*2. Avoid snacking between meals, and eat fewer meals.* Disciplining your desire to eat is the first and most important step toward insuring proper digestion and elimination of food. Next, you must understand that the human body was not designed for constant eating. We are not like cows which must consume tremendous volumes of grass each day to survive, and so must be eating during much of their waking lives. To be honest, a perfectly healthy adult human being whose organs are all functioning properly does best with a single meal a day and liquids the rest of the time. For most of us, however, two or even three meals per day seem to be required. (People with certain conditions like hypoglycemia may require food more often.)

The important thing is that the stomach and other digestive organs need a rest between meals. Digestion requires energy, and that energy must be drawn from other parts of the body. If you snack between meals, then either your brain and your muscles will be deprived of the energy they need to do their work, or your digestive organs will not receive the energy necessary to do their jobs, and digestion will be sluggish or incomplete.

Another thing to consider is that your digestive and eliminative organs use the time when they are not processing

23

your food to "do their housekeeping." Partially digested bits of food or fecal matter are removed from these organs so that they can be in prime condition when it comes time to eat again. But if you don't give them a break between meals, then the waste matter accumulates and can, over a period of years, encumber those organs to such an extent that you cannot properly draw the nutrients from your food and eliminate waste. Inevitably, disease results.

*3. Eat only when hungry.* We have already discussed some of the reasons for not eating impulsively. We must take it a step farther and say, even if you are scheduled to eat a meal, don't eat unless you're hungry, and don't eat if you're emotionally upset. When you have no appetite, your body may be trying to tell you something. Perhaps, for reasons unknown to you, your last meal did not digest properly. We have all seen how dogs and cats, when they are not well, immediately stop eating. They follow the dictates of their bodies and not of the clock. If you are not hungry at meal time, then you should stop and reflect on your activities of the day and on your overall physical condition. It may be a clue that your diet needs to be altered, or that you should slow down and rest to avoid illness.

*4. Chew well; your stomach has no teeth.* It may seem obvious, but your teeth cut and grind your food so that it is easier for your stomach to digest. In the case of many raw vegetables, vital nutrients are not released from the fiber unless they are cut and ground in this way. While you chew, the food is digested by the saliva in the mouth. These digestive juices are not duplicated in the stomach. That's why even raw fruit and vegetable juices need to be "chewed." When you swallow your food without giving it a good chew, you may be losing your only opportunity to get the nourishment out of it.

*5. Stop eating when you're three-fourths full.* Most of us have been conditioned to eat and eat "until we can't eat another bite." Perhaps this habit is a holdover from generations ago when our ancestors did not have enough to eat. It seemed to make sense to them that they should stuff themselves when a good solid meal came along. After all, they might not see a good meal again for weeks or months. But few people reading this book ever go hungry. Eating until we are about to burst is both unnecessary and unhealthful.

Think of your stomach as a vessel in which a chemical reaction is about to occur. That chemical reaction is the process of digestion. Food and liquid are the reagents which participate in the reaction. As is the case with many chemical reactions, a certain amount of gas is released as the food digests. Now if you fill a sealed vessel with reagents and gas is suddenly released, you may have an explosion. In your case, you'll probably just get a stomach ache. So, when you eat, fill your stomach with two parts of food, one part of liquid, but allow a quarter of your stomach's capacity to remain free for digestion.

6. *Rest after every meal.* In simpler times, it was expected that people would rest for a while after every meal. There was no pressure to "eat and run." It is, in fact, a sign of good food and proper digestion to feel sleepy after a meal. It means that your body is withdrawing its energy from other body systems and applying them to digestion. You may even experience a "chilly" feeling after a good meal, like you want to crawl under a warm blanket and take a nap. That's also a good sign. Don't fight it. Take ten minutes for a short nap, or if that's impossible, at least sit quietly for a while and relax. The renewed vitality which you feel when you resume your regular activities will more than compensate for the slight delay.

7. *Don't eat after sunset,* or at least not just before bed. In ancient times, when people lived by the sun, they were instructed not to eat after sunset. This is what it says in the ancient scriptures. But for modern man, who lives by the clock, this may not be feasible. The basic principle, however, can still be applied. Like thinking and exercising, sleeping is a unique activity which should not have to compete with digestion. Sleep is a time of healing and rejuvenation for the entire body. Proper digestion

does not occur during this period. Especially once the food has passed beyond the stomach, the intestines and the colon rely upon the movement of our bodies during our waking hours to help them do their work. That is why a sedentary lifestyle often leads to constipation. Imagine the effect of eating a large meal shortly before entering into a nearly motionless sleep.

Ideally, one should allow at least four hours between the last meal of the day and bedtime. Under no circumstances should you go to bed within two hours of your final meal. If you must eat late in the day, take these suggestions: Eat lightly. A simple meal of fruit or steamed vegetables digests far more quickly than a four-course Italian dinner, and you'll awaken in the morning feeling light and refreshed. Secondly, take a long walk before bed. It will help prevent the intestinal tract from getting clogged.

*8. Eat only what you can eliminate within twenty-four hours.* Many people have been taught that as long as they have a bowel movement every day or so they are not constipated. Actually, it is not so much the frequency of one's stools that is important as the period of time it takes for the food to pass out of one's body.

The colon can be compared to a pipe leading to a sewer or a septic tank. It was not designed to serve as a toxic waste dump. Unfortunately, when our food remains in our bodies for longer than twenty-four hours, that is what the colon becomes. The waste begins to putrefy, and harmful toxins are absorbed back into the system. The liver, whose job it is to remove toxins from the bloodstream, can become overloaded, and then the entire body becomes contaminated. This condition is called *autotoxemia.* Symptoms of auto-toxemia include impaired appetite, lack of energy, lackluster eyes and skin, a coated tongue and foul breath. Malaise, headaches, irritability and nervousness are also common.

Constipation can have many causes: overeating, a diet too high in processed foods, lack of exercise, or even anxiety. But the most common cause of constipation in our society is the consumption of meat and other animal products. Meat, fish, fowl and eggs simply do not digest within twenty-four hours. A similar problem is created by eating too much hard cheese. Yogi Bhajan often tells his students, "Don't eat anything which runs away, flies away or swims away when you try to catch it." The problem with cheese is, it just sits there! And it sits in your intestinal tract too. Many vegetarians who have recently given up meat fall into the trap of eating lots of hard cheese. True, cheese is very tasty, and it lends a feeling of "substance" to a vegetable meal which former meat-eaters often find lacking. The best advice is, if you must eat hard cheese, eat less. Have one slice in your cheese sandwich, not two. And as for pizza and other cheesy delights, once or twice a week is okay, but don't make it your regular diet.

How do you know whether you are eliminating your food within twenty-four hours? A simple test is to prepare a meal with lots of beets. Record the time when it was eaten and wait. The beets will dye your stool a deep red. When that meal comes out, you will know. *There are several remedies for simple constipation in Chapter Ten.* But for severe chronic problems, a complete change of diet and perhaps a visit to your doctor may be necessary.


*9. Once a week, give your digestive system a rest.* We have already described how our digestive organs use the periods between meals to do their "housekeeping." For optimum health, a more thorough rest once a week is in order. Not only does a day off from eating give your internal organs a rest, it also breaks the "food habit" so that it is easier to regulate your diet during the rest of the week. Your day off can be in the form of a complete water fast, a day of drinking only liquids, or a day of eating only light foods like fruits. What you choose will probably depend on your ability to sustain a short fast and your ability to carry out your required duties while fasting. If even a one-day fast seems impossible to you, then try skipping one meal, and then two, until you are more used to the feeling of not eating. *For a more thorough discussion of fasting, see Chapter Nine.*

*10. If you can't digest it and eliminate it, don't eat it.* After reading the preceding nine guidelines, perhaps this should go without saying. Nonetheless, some people literally eat themselves to death because they have been unwilling to break bad habits, even when the consequences have been clearly shown to them. Many people feel that it is their "right" to eat the foods they enjoy, and their egos bristle when anyone suggests that they temporarily give up their favorite foods. That may be true, but it is also their right to be healthy. It is a simple question of which is more important.

Even if you are eating a perfect vegetarian diet with fresh foods and all the vitamins and minerals your body needs, you still may not be able to digest it. One way of checking yourself is to examine your stools. Ideally, they should be composed of equal amounts of solid waste and air. That should make them float in the water. If your stools are sinking, you are sinking! Your food is not being thoroughly digested. The thing to do is to go on a diet of "predigested food" like *Mung Beans and Rice* until the condition is corrected and your stools float once again. Assess yourself, be honest, and then use the information in this book to correct your unhealthy conditions.

## Chapter Five:

# Foods for Health
## & Healing

In this chapter we'll take a break from our guidelines for healthful living and look at some of the most common foods and their health-giving properties. Read this chapter from beginning to end, skip around, or use it as a reference. There are more tips for personal health, hygiene and diet beginning in Chapter Six.

### ALMONDS

The almond is a wonderful nut. It can be eaten whole, or made into butter or milk. Its oil is excellent for both internal and external use. In most cases, the outside skin, which is very astringent, should be removed before using. *See Chapter Seven for special uses of almonds for women. Also "Ms. Whiz."*

Almonds are an excellent source of protein for vegetarians. (Three to six ounces contain as much protein as a truly healthy person needs in a day.) Almonds are a good source of manganese, phosphorus and potassium. They are easily digestible and good for the eyes. *See Golden Fig-Nut Chutney, Nut Curry Supreme, Potency Potion, Saffron Almond Rice, Trinity Saffron Nut Spread and Weight-Gain Pie.*

Almond Milk *(See "Children's Recipes" — Chapter Eight)* is an excellent first food for babies, and is also good for those suffering from anemia, diabetes and malnutrition.

Young children should not eat almonds whole. Instead, give them Almond Butter. *(See "Special Foods for Children" — Chapter Eight)*. It can be used as a tasty spread for the entire family.

Mixed with lemon water to form a paste, almond butter can be used as a natural cosmetic. Spread it on your lips and allow it to sit for a few minutes. Then rinse with warm water. It will make your lips red and glossy.

Almond oil is one of the best things for body care. At night, wash your feet with cold water. Then stand in a tub of hot water for a few minutes. A lot of blood will go to your feet, vitalizing the whole body. Then massage your feet with almond oil, wrap a cotton cloth around them, put on some big socks, and go to sleep. In the morning, wash your feet with warm water (and no soap). It's the best beauty treatment for your feet.

## APPLES

Apples are believed to have originated in the Middle East near the site of the biblical "Garden of Eden." Today the apple is one of the most common fruits and one of the best. Everyone knows the expression, "An apple a day keeps the doctor away." Apples are body cleansers and blood purifiers. They are high in sodium, potassium, magnesium and vitamins B and C. An apple in the morning will strengthen the body. Eaten at the end of a meal it will aid in digestion. Apples are beneficial cooked or raw. They are cleansing any way you prepare them. Two or three baked apples eaten just before going to sleep will help relieve and prevent constipation. A diet of baked apples and cottage cheese will cleanse and renew the blood. They are also an excellent food for children. *See "Children's Recipes" — Chapter Eight. Also Dried Honey Apples and Weight-Gain Pie.*

## BANANAS

The Latin name for banana is *musa sapientum*, which means "fruit of the wise men." The name comes from an ancient traveler's tale which says that the sages of India rested in the shade of the banana plant's broad leaves as they discussed religion and philosophy. It is indeed a wise person today who eats this beautiful yellow fruit. Bananas are a good energy food. They are high in phosphorus and potassium and are good for the whole family. They are especially good for a woman, since they provide her with the minerals and nutrients her body and nervous system needs. The white stringy pulp on the inside of the peel should be scraped off and eaten too. It is good for balancing the metals in the body and for its Vitamin A content. Bananas can help stop both constipation and diarrhea. For diarrhea eat one banana every three hours, and for constipation eat three bananas every hour until these conditions change. Neither unripe nor overripe fruit should be eaten. A banana is ripe when all traces of green are gone from the peel and brown or black spots have begun to appear. When the dark spots grow large and soft to the touch, then the banana has become overripe. *For revitalizing the body, see "Banana Fast" in Chapter Nine. Also see Banana-Nutmeg Icecream, Coconut Icecream, Ms. Whiz, and Split Milk Shake.*

## BEETS

Beets can't be beat for being healthy. They cleanse the liver and the intestinal tract. For the liver, cook beets (with or without the greens) along with carrots, herbs and spices for a delicious and healthful meal. *(See Beet-Carrot Casserole.)* Beet juice is good for the liver too, but it is best taken in small quantities in combination with other juices. *(See "Liver" — Chapter Ten.)*

Beets can be used either for gaining or for losing weight. For quick weight gain, eat steamed beets with cottage cheese or tofu as well as crushed almonds and baked apples. *(See Weight-Gain Pie.)* To lose weight, go on a mono diet of beets and beet greens.

Beets can be used in the treatment of hemorrhoids, to eliminate toxins from the body, and to regulate the body's sugar balance.

## BLACK PEPPER

A small dried berry, black pepper is the most popular spice in the world, and a very beneficial food. When freshly ground, it is an effective blood purifier. It aids in the digestion of food, and forces out gas from the bottom of the stomach. Sprinkled on melons, it prevents the formation of intestinal gas. When taken in large quantities, it will make a person sweat. An Indian flat bread made with ground black pepper can be used to break a fever. (*See Spiced Chapatis.*) By boiling a half teaspoon of whole peppercorns in water for five minutes, you can make a tea which is useful in treating arthritis and asthma. *Also see Celery Pancakes, Weight-Loss Tea, and Yogi Tea.*

## CELERY

The classical Greek medical writer, Dioscorides, recommended eating celery for its sedative effect. In fact, celery is very soothing to the nervous system, and drinking celery juice is a sure way to calm the nerves. (Don't put salt in celery juice, since it can cause diarrhea.) Celery is also a good internal cleanser. Its stringy fibers work like brushes on the walls of the intestines. The celery heart is a food which protects against heart attack. *See Celery Pancakes, Sesame Yogurt Dressing and Yogi Mush.*

## CHILES

When Columbus arrived in America, the native peoples were using chile in their daily diets. Misnamed "pepper" by those seeking the black pepper of India, they are members of the nightshade family, along with tomatoes, potatoes and eggplant. All chiles and other so-called "peppers" belong to the group called *capsicum.* Green and red chile in the form of dry chile flakes, cayenne powder and fresh whole green jalapenos or serranos are powerful healing foods. Chiles are extremely high in vitamin C and A. They are beneficial to the circulatory and digestive systems. In spite of their hot and pungent taste chiles have a soothing effect on the system. They have even been used as a cure for ulcers and to stop hemorraging.

You should always be careful when preparing hot chiles for they can literally burn the skin and eyes. Chiles are hot because they contain capsaicin, an acid. The more capsaicin, the hotter the chile. Most of this hot element is found in the pulpy core and the seeds which are attached to it. To cool down a chile, these can be removed. If you do get burned by a chile, internally or externally, rather than using water use milk, and for extreme cases use baking soda to neutralize the capsaicin. Remember, hot chiles hurt going in and coming out of the body, so be moderate in their use until you are used to them. Once you have grown used to eating chiles, however, you'll not want to eat a meal without them. *See Anti-Smog Pancakes, Chiles and Cheese, Jalapeno Milk, Nut Curry Supreme, and Solstice Hot Sauce.*

## COCONUT

The coconut is one of the most healthful and nutritious foods available. It is a real body-builder, useful in gaining weight. Its protein contains all the essential amino acids, and its oil is easily digestible. A one hundred-year-old man in India has lived his last seventy-five years on coconuts alone. Their milk is rich in easily assimilated protein, vitamin C and B-complex, and a long list of minerals. A refreshing summer beverage, it is good for bones and teeth, and is useful in the treatment of urinary diseases, constipation, vomiting, fatigue, nervousness and general weakness. Coconut meat is an ancient cure for intestinal worms. *Also see Coconut Icecream.*

## DATES

The date palm was sacred to many ancient peoples. Some scholars believe that the biblical "Tree of Life" in the Garden of Eden was really a date palm. The skins of the date provide roughage which makes the date an excellent laxative. It is also useful in treating dysentery. Because date sugar is not as harmful to the teeth as other sugars, dates are a good substitute for candy. They are also a healthful snack when you need quick energy. *Datemilk* is a nourishing, youth-maintaining beverage which can be served to young and old alike. It is especially helpful in recovering from a fever.

*33*

# GARLIC

Throughout the ancient world, garlic was considered a sacred and powerful herb. In the modern era, science has been confirming its marvelous healing properties. Known in the Soviet Union as "Russian penicillin," garlic oil has been found to be a natural antibiotic. Garlic and garlic extracts have been used against gastrointestinal disorders, septic poisoning, typhus, cholera, bacterial infections and even cancer. It is also a stimulant to the sexual system. It promotes the production of semen, and is thus a vital addition to any man's diet. Most effective when eaten raw, it is available in capsule form for those who find its odor socially embarrassing. When cooked with onion and ginger (see "Trinity Roots" — this chapter) it has a very healthful effect. Also see Garlic Toast, Saffron Almond Rice and Sesame Yogurt Dressing.

# GHEE

In the medical writings of ancient India, ghee is highly regarded as both a nutrient and a preservative for foods and medicines. Ghee is also called "clarified butter" because the impurities have been removed. A dish cooked in it retains its freshness and nutritional value much longer. Ghee will keep unrefrigerated for several weeks, is very low in cholesterol, and is much healthier than butter. Moreover, it can be heated to a higher temperature than butter without burning, and is therefore a healthful cooking oil. You will find many uses for ghee throughout this book. To find out how to make Ghee, see Recipes.

# GINGER

Ginger has been used as both a medicine and a spice for thousands of years. At one time it was actually worth its weight in gold. Ginger root nourishes the nervous system, allowing it to carry more energy. It is both soothing and strengthening to the nerves when the body is under stress, and is especially helpful to women during menstruation. It has been used for backaches, fatigue, flu, fevers, bronchial coughs, and as a digestive stimulant. Yogic tradition holds that it is nourishing to the cerebrospinal fluid and "draws out wind from the spinal column." Ginger can be sauteed or boiled in water to make tea. It is one of the "trinity roots," along with onion and garlic. Cooked together, these three roots form the basis of many healing recipes. *See Golden Fig Nut Chutney and Sesame-Ginger Milk.*

## GRAPES

This delicious fruit is excellent for purifying the blood and rebuilding the body. Grapes are a good source of vitamin C, magnesium and potassium. Eaten as a mono diet, they can be used to totally transform the bloodstream and detoxify the body to overcome chronic diseases. Grapes are a natural laxative. Green grapes can be eaten for a clear complexion.

## HONEY AND BEE POLLEN

Honey is a wonderful food, but no more than one ounce (two tablespoons) per day is recommended. Honey has been used as a treatment for a wide array of ailments, including asthma, hay fever, allergies, digestive disorders, arthritis, multiple sclerosis, hemorrhoids, bad complexion and a weak heart. It improves assimilation and elimination and is good for longevity. Honey increases calcium retention and rejuvenates the female reproductive system. Bee pollen, which shares the benefits of honey in a concentrated form, is available in tablets, capsules, or in bulk. A recommended daily dosage is 10 tablets, 4-6 capsules, or 1 tablespoon. *See Dried Honey Apples.*

## LECITHIN

Lecithin is an oil found in soybeans. It is found in the brain and is a coating for the nerves. It helps in the conductivity of nerve impulses. Taken daily, it has been found to improve the memory and aid overall mental functioning. Lecithin has the unique property of combining with fats in the bloodstream and along artery walls. It is thus helpful in cases of high blood pressure, heart problems and poor circulation. It has been useful in clearing skin conditions and in stimulating the growth of hair. It is essential for the production of semen. Lecithin is best taken in liquid form, two or three tablespoons daily. If larger doses are taken, take calcium lactate to balance the excess phosphorus in the lecithin.

## LEGUMES

The family of legumes, or *dhal* as it is called in India, includes beans, peas, lentils and so on. Combined with grains such as rice, wheat or corn, they form a complete protein and the foundation of a vegetarian diet. Dried beans and peas build up the hemoglobin content of the blood. Sprouted legumes, especially lentils and mung beans, can be cooked or eaten raw in salads. Mung beans are among the healthiest, most nourishing and easiest to digest of the legumes. They are a wonderful food for those doing spiritual practices. Cooked together with rice and vegetables they are a complete, predigested food on which you could live the rest of your life. All dry legumes should be presoaked and well cooked to be easily digested. *See Mung Beans and Rice.*

## LEMONS

An excellent source of vitamin C, calcium, potassium and magnesium, lemons were once considered more of a medicine than a food. Lemons purify the blood by stirring up acids for elimination. Though lemons are acidic, their effect on the blood is alkalinizing. They are useful in treating liver disorders. In the case of a sore throat, cold or fever, dissolve lemon juice and honey in hot water for a soothing drink. This same drink is useful for breaking a fast, or for cleansing the throat and stomach of mucus upon waking. *See Nut Curry Supreme, Saffron Almond Rice and Weight-Loss Tea.*

# MANGOES

There are over thirty varieties of mango growing in tropical climates throughout the world. The best mangoes are bright orange in color. They are helpful in correcting liver disorders and menstrual disorders, and are great for people who need to gain weight. When you eat mangoes, always drink milk to balance their acidity. A mono diet of mangoes and milk will greatly improve health and vigor. It has also been useful in cases of poor eyesight, constipation, indigestion and sexual weakness. To follow this diet, eat eight to ten large mangoes with eight cups of milk per day. *Also see Mango Lassi.*

# MUSTARD GREENS

Mustard greens are extremely high in calcium, Vitamins A and Vitamin C. They are one of the most healthful vegetables consumed. The chlorophyll in them builds and purifies the blood. They are especially good when cooked together with ghee, *paneer,* spices and herbs in the form of *saag. See Saag Paneer.*

# ONIONS

The onion derives its name from the Latin word *unus,* meaning "one." Its divine architecture of concentric spheres led the ancient Egyptians to regard the onion as the symbol of the universe. If there is any such thing as a "universal" healing food, it is the onion. It has been prescribed for a long list of ailments including: earache, colds, fever, dizziness, laryngitis, diarrhea, insomnia, vomiting and warts. Its primary effect is on the blood. It stimulates the production of blood and purifies the blood by attacking any bacteria which are harmful to the body. Although no food is a complete safeguard against cancer, onions are among the best cancer preventive foods. "An onion a day keeps the cancer away." Raw onions in the diet aid in mental clarity. Eaten daily for two weeks before travelling abroad, they can help to prevent dysentery.

Onions are said to create heat and add energy to the body. They are helpful in cleansing the liver, digesting food, and eliminating mucus. Raw onions are the most effective. However they should not be eaten by people with ulcers, colitis or high blood pressure. Cooked onions are less effective, but they are still very healthful. Boiled onions are a natural laxative. Onions, garlic and ginger comprise the "trinity roots." Cooked together, their healing properties are greatly increased. *See Parsley Pilau, Pistachio Paranthas, Sesame Yogurt Dressing and Solstice Hot Sauce.*

## ORANGES

The orange is an acidic fruit which, like the lemon, has an alkalinizing effect on the blood. Oranges cleanse the blood by stirring up acids and mucus for elimination. They have been found helpful in cases of asthma, high blood pressure and ailments of the heart and liver. Everyone knows that oranges are high in vitamin C. They are also a good source of potassium, calcium, sodium and magnesium. When eating an orange, eat the white lining of the peel as well. It is good for balancing the minerals in the body. *See "Ms. Whiz."*

## PANEER

"Paneer" is the Indian name for homemade cottage cheese. It is less fattening and easier to digest than the cottage cheese we buy in the supermarket. Whey is a byproduct of making paneer which makes a healthful drink or cooking ingredient. Also referred to as "curds and whey," paneer and whey are two of the best foods to serve to children. *For instructions on how to make them, see recipe for Paneer. Also see Saag Paneer.*

## PAPAYA

The papaya is a heavenly fruit. It is especially soothing to the stomach and intestinal tract. In fact, it contains the digestive enzyme papain. Its milky juice has been drunk through the ages as a treatment for warts, eczema, intestinal worms and ulcers. It is rich in vitamins A, B, C and D, and in calcium. It is also an excellent food for young children.

The inside skin of the papaya has been used as a beauty treatment. Rub it on your face, allow it to dry, then rinse for a beautiful complexion. Its seeds are useful too. Dry them and grind them into a powder. Use as a seasoning like pepper.

Hawaiian papayas are ripe and ready to eat when the skins are yellow or orange and the fruit is a little soft. The large variety, which is mostly available from Mexico, is ripe when most of the green is gone from the outside, having changed to yellow or orange. It is very tasty with lemon juice. *Also see "Melon Diet" — Chapter Nine.*

## PARSLEY

In America, parsley is a food which is served as a decoration on every plate, but it is seldom eaten. This is unfortunate, because parsley is really a wonderful food. It is rich in minerals, and is useful in building the blood. It has been helpful in treating diabetes, in cleansing the kidneys, and in regulating the calcium balance in the body. It is also an excellent breath freshener. (Have some parsley after you've been eating garlic.) Parsley juice can be used for purging the body of poisons. *See Parsley Pilau and Yogi Mush.*

## PINEAPPLE

This tropical fruit has a very invigorating effect on the curative forces of the body. When the liver or the kidneys are overstressed, pineapple juice can give them the boost they need. Because of its high chlorine content, pineapple juice can be used to purge the body of wastes by stimulating urination. Pineapple juice is very soothing to the throat and is very helpful for singers. Fortunately, canned or bottled pineapple juice seems to have all the curative properties of fresh juice. *See Potent Potatoes.*

# POTATOES

The potato is one of the most nourishing vegetables. It is high in protein, vitamins A and B and alkaline salts. These alkaline salts are useful in neutralizing acid wastes and cleansing body tissues. Potatoes must be cooked in order to be properly digested. To get the greatest nutritional value from your potatoes, boil them whole with the skins intact. When you cut them up before cooking, you lose about one-third of the nutrients. You should also eat potatoes with their skins. The skin is very alkaline, providing a balance for the acid whites of the potato. Avoid potatoes that have sprouted, or those that have been exposed to sunlight and turned green; they may be poisonous. Potatoes are useful in ridding the body of toxins such as uric acid. A cup of potato peel broth each morning may be helpful in loosening up stiff joints due to rheumatism or arthritis. *See Parsley Pilau and Potent Potatoes.*


# RICE

Rice is a native of India, where it has grown since before the beginning of recorded history. It is revered throughout Asia as a sacred food.

Most of the rice we eat in the West is milled, or "polished." That is what gives it its snow-white color. Milling or "polishing" rice can strip away ten percent of its protein, eighty-five percent of its fat, and seventy percent of its minerals, as well as a large part of the B vitamins it contains. For this reason, many health-conscious vegetarians eat brown rice, which is unpolished . However, Yogi Bhajan warns that brown rice which has been grown in the mineral-poor soil of America must be thoroughly cooked — perhaps for as long as twenty-four hours — with plenty of water so as not to be unhealthful.

For this reason, it is preferable to use Basmati rice or Mexican unpolished rice. While most white rice has been polished, Basmati rice, an Indian variety, is a fragrant and high-quality rice which is naturally white without milling. It is abundant in B vitamins, iodine and high-quality protein and is easily assimilated. All rice, however, should be cooked with plenty of water until tender so as to be easily digestible.

Rice isn't fattening. In fact, a diet of Basmati rice cooked with lemon juice and turmeric will melt the pounds away and leave you healthy and glowing. Rice stimulates the kidneys so that toxins are eliminated and urination is increased. Rice with curry is very good for the kidneys, blood purification and muscle development. *See Mung Beans and Rice, Parsley Pilau, Saffron Almond Rice, Trinity Rice and Yogurt Curry. Also see "Children's Recipes" for Basmati Rice Soup — Chapter Eight.*

## SESAME SEEDS

The sesame is the most potent of all seeds. Sesame seeds increase virility, rejuvenate mental and physical capacity and endurance, and increase the secretions of the pituitary, pineal and sex glands. They are good for the brain and nerve tissue as well. They contain abundant potassium and magnesium, and are an excellent source of lecithin.

The only problem with sesame seeds is that they are hard to digest raw. Roasted, they are easily digestible, but they lose sixty percent of their food value. So when you buy roasted sesame seeds, you are really wasting a lot of money! What to do? One way to prepare sesame seeds so that they are easy to digest while preserving most of their nutritional value is to mix them into chapati dough in the ratio of one part seeds to three parts dough. Then add vegetables and make a nice stuffed *chapati.* Another way is to blend the sesame seeds at a low speed (so you don't heat them) with a little-water to make sesame butter. This can be used as a spread, or cooked into sourdough bread for a delicious treat. *See Sesame Sourdough Bread. Also see Sesame Ginger Milk and Sesame Yogurt Dressing.*

41

# TRINITY ROOTS

Onion, garlic and ginger, the "trinity roots," will maintain you through the times. These tasty roots are essential to a healthy diet for cleansing, producing and sustaining energy in the body. While each of these roots is beneficial when taken alone, cooking them together causes them to interact, amplifying their effect on the body. Onions purify the blood and stimulate the production of semen. Garlic enhances semen production and maintains potency. The seminal fluid is reabsorbed into the spine to nourish the brain and the nervous system with the aid of ginger. When this happens, one is able to fight off disease; he becomes creatively very effective; and he can look forward to a long and healthy life. Now trinity roots are available in capsule form. *See "Where To Find It" at the back of this book.* Trinity roots form the basis for many of our healing recipes. *For more information about trinity roots, see separate sections on garlic, ginger and onions in this chapter. Also see Anti-smog Pancakes, Nut Curry Supreme, Mung Beans and Rice, Potent Potatoes, Trinity Rice, Trinity Saffron Nut Spread and Yogurt Curry.*

# TURMERIC

Turmeric is a root which is ground into a bright yellow powder. It is one of the main ingredients in curry powder and gives it its color. In the West, it is used to color prepared mustard. However, turmeric is a health-giving food which has been recognized as such in India for centuries. Current research in India indicates that it may, as long thought, be of value in preventing diabetes and cancer. Its primary use is as a "lubricant" to make the joints flexible. It is also excellent for the skin and for the mucous membranes, especially the female reproductive organs.

Turmeric should always be cooked before eating. If you wish, you can cook it in water or oil to make a paste and then save that paste to use in various recipes. One precaution about turmeric: it will stain. Wash the stain immediately and leave out in the sun. *See Eggplant Pakoras, Nut Curry Supreme, Parsley Pilau, Potent Potatoes, Saffron Almond Rice, Solstice Hot Sauce and Yogurt Curry.*

# WATERCRESS

Watercress has been used as a food for thousands of years. This green-leafed salad vegetable was fed to children in ancient Persia to improve their growth. The ancient Greeks believed it had the power to cure a deranged mind. Watercress is high in minerals, including sulfur, chlorine and calcium. It is good for those with high blood pressure. Helpful in reducing water retention, it is a natural diuretic.

# WATERMELON

Watermelon is a very therapeutic food which is often taken for granted. It is a perfect food, especially for children, when the weather is very hot. It is a very good food to fast on. It is better than water, because the fibers of the melon act like little brushes to clean the intestines. Meanwhile, the watermelon sugar gives you energy to keep going. It can be used for the relief of intestinal gas, and for cleansing the liver. To avoid intestinal gas, it is best to eat watermelon sprinkled with black pepper. Watermelon juice is also good for you, especially if you think you are getting a cold. You can eat the seeds, which are high in vitamin E, or cook them into your meals. *See Nut Curry Supreme and Saffron Almond Rice.*

## WHEAT

Wheat has correctly been called the staff of life. The whole wheatberry, from which wheat flour is milled, is an excellent food when boiled until tender. It cleans the intestinal tract, gives strong teeth and gums, beautifies the skin, and can prevent stomach problems, including cancer. It stores well, and is thus an excellent "survival food." However, you must accustom your system to wheatberries gradually. So one day a week, fast on wheatberries. You can eat them with milk and a little honey. Your body will thank you for it.

When cooked, or soaked overnight, wheatberries can be blended to form wheat milk. This is an excellent nourishing food for children too young to eat whole grains. *See "Children's Recipes" for Wheat Milk and Wheatberry Cream — Chapter Eight.*

Wheat, in the form of bread, is a "brain food." There are leavened breads, unleavened breads, and fried Indian breads like chapatis, *puris* and paranthas. By adding various fruits, vegetables, herbs and spices to the dough before cooking, these breads become powerful healing foods. *See Fruit Bran Bread, Pistachio Paranthas, Sesame Sourdough Bread and Spiced Chapatis. Also "Children's Recipes" for Zweiback — Chapter Eight.*

Wheat Bran, which is the outer husk of the wheat, is a most valuable substance. It is high in lime, iron, B-complex vitamins and potash. It contains lots of cellulose which is helpful in avoiding constipation, and can be used as a natural laxative. Whereas wheat flour is acid-forming, bran is alkalinizing, neutralizing the effect of the wheat when the two are prepared together. *Bran tea* can be made by boiling bran with six times its weight in water for thirty minutes. Honey or lemon can be added to taste. It is a natural remedy for nervousness, anemia, hoarseness and sore throats. Drink one cup twice a day. *Also see Fruit Bran Bread.*

## YOGI TEA

Though it is really a combination of foods, *Yogi Tea* is so important in the diet Yogi Bhajan recommends to his students that it is included in this chapter. Yogi tea is a delicous drink which acts as a mild stimulant. It is a healthful substitute for coffee or strong black tea. It can give you a nice "high" while your feet stay firmly planted on the ground.

Yogi tea, when regularly included in the diet, helps to correct damage done to the nervous system by drugs. Actually, it is a tonic to the nervous system. It will improve your memory and balance you out when you're feeling out of balance. It can take away tiredness and bring you out of discouragement and depression. It can give you the energy to achieve your goals. Yogi tea is both a remedy and a preventive measure for colds, flu and diseases of the mucous membranes.

The ingredients of yogi tea are divine. Black pepper is a blood purifier. Cardamon is for the colon. Together, they support the brain cells. Cloves are for the nervous system. Cinnamon is for the bones. Ginger adds flavor, is strengthening to the nervous system, and is very good if you are suffering from a cold, flu or any physical weakness. Milk aids in the assimilation of the spices, and avoids irritation to the colon and stomach. The black tea in the recipe acts as a catalyst for all the other ingredients. Please note: the black tea *is necessary.* Herb tea will not work in its place. Also, Yogi Tea should not be served without milk. For complete directions, *see Recipes.*

45

# YOGURT

Homemade yogurt is a food to be eaten every day. It is rich in vitamin B-12, which is essential for the nervous system. Since the body cannot manufacture vitamin B-12 from vegetable sources, yogurt is an important element in vegetarian nutrition. It is a natural cleanser of the stomach and intestines. It neutralizes acidic conditions and enriches the intestinal flora. When the intestinal flora is depleted, as is often the case after taking antibiotics, a regular diet of homemade yogurt will help restore it again. Homemade yogurt is an excellent shampoo, a superb deep cleanser for the body, and an effective douche.

Why homemade yogurt and not the store-bought kind? The active agents in yogurt from which we derive most benefit are *Lactobacillus acidophilus* bacteria. They are "friendly" bacteria which aid in digestion and actually destroy various "unfriendly" bacteria. While some commercial yogurts are better than others, most do not allow the bacteria in yogurt to multiply to the extent that you can when you make it at home. The longer you let your yogurt sit at room temperature before refrigerating, the stronger the bacteria cultures will become. A very strong acidophilus yogurt "drink" is very therapeutic for some conditions. Most commercial yogurts, even those made without gum, gelatin or stabilizers, add milk solids to thicken the yogurt. This makes the yogurt a concentrated food which is more difficult to digest. *For directions for making your own yogurt, see Homemade Yogurt. Also see Mango Lassi, Nut Curry Supreme, Saffron Almond Rice, Sesame Yogurt Dressing and Yogurt Curry.*

*Chapter Six:*

# Foods for Men

Contrary to popular opinion, men and women are very different creatures. While they share many similarities of biology, important differences in the structure of their brains and the powerful impact of their hormonal and sexual makeups cause them to experience very different realities in the realm of consciousness. These differences also require that they eat somewhat different foods and adopt different eating habits.

Before a man eats, four conditions should be met. First, he should be surrounded by a calm and quiet atmosphere. Second, he should be free of any mental or physical pressure. Third, the food he is about to eat should be properly prepared from proper ingredients. And last, there should be enough time for him to eat gracefully. If these conditions do not exist, it is better for a man to remain hungry. Even the best food, eaten under stressful conditions, will put pressure on a man's nervous system which is worse for his constitution than not eating at all.

## FOOD AND SEX

Speaking "man to man," when your relationship with the woman in your life is not right, nothing is right. When your communication with your mate is bad, you will feel overtaxed by your work and you will not feel relaxed. To minimize the negative effects on your system, there are three things you should do right away: Cut down on your total intake of food. You'll live longer.

Next, cut out all heavy foods from your diet. This includes all animal proteins, hard cheese, fatty foods, and anything else that doesn't digest easily. Finally, cut out all stimulating drinks. This means sugar-sweetened drinks, alcoholic beverages, and caffeine drinks like coffee, tea and cola. Following these recommendations may not bring instant harmony to your love life, but it will make the difficult periods less of a strain on your body and mind.

One of the biggest causes of sexual dysfunction in men is the habit of filling their stomachs more than three-fourths full at mealtimes. The basic reasons for not eating until completely full were discussed in Chapter Four, but for men this bad habit can result in additional problems. Temporary impotency is a condition that usually develops around age thirty-six, but sometimes as early as age twenty-seven. It commonly occurs in men who habitually eat and eat until they can eat no more. Then they are surprised to find that, at an early age, they cannot function sexually. If this is the problem, then the remedy is simple. For a few weeks, go on a liquid diet of juices and soups — nothing concentrated. Then resume a normal diet of healthful, nutritious food, being careful to always eat in moderation.

About the worst thing a man can do to his health is to engage in sexual intercourse after eating. The sexual act is very heavy exercise involving all your muscles, your mind and your entire nervous system. Having sex after eating can ruin your stomach, and if you do so often, can lead to premature ejaculation. For optimal sexual function, a man should eat nothing but liquids all day prior to sexual intercourse. However, an interval of four hours between eating and sex is adequate. In no case should a man engage in sexual intercourse within two and a half hours after a meal.

Following sexual intercourse (not immediately following, but after a period of sleep), it is advisable for a man to take special foods to strengthen his nervous system and replenish his sexual fluids. For this purpose, *Yogi Tea, Sesame-Ginger Milk,* and warm milk with sesame oil are excellent.

The food a man eats affects not only his health but his potency as well. According to the ancient yogic system of health, potency is not just a matter of adequate sexual function. It is that and more. Potency is the inner capacity of a man to project outward — it is his creativity and effectiveness. Potency is based upon many factors — physical, mental and spiritual — and has an impact in each of these realms. One of the most important factors contributing to potency is the presence of a high level of good quality semen in the body. Yogic science teaches that semen is not just sexual fluid for reproduction. It is a lubricant for the brain and the nervous system, like oil in an automobile engine. If your semen is plentiful and "high-grade," you will have more resistance to the "heat" of physical and mental pressure than you would otherwise. You can be your own man, and more effectively accomplish your goals in life despite any obstacles. According to yogic theory, it takes eighty bites of food to produce a drop of blood, and eighty drops of blood to produce a drop of semen. With this in mind, a man should value his sexual fluid, and include in his diet those foods which stimulate the production of this precious liquid. See *Potency Potion and Sesame-Ginger Milk*.

## SPECIAL FOODS FOR MEN

The following foods are especially useful for men in increasing their potency, correcting sexual dysfunctions, and preserving their sexual vigor:

*Banyan Tree Milk*. The sap of the banyan tree can correct many imbalances in the male sexual system. It strengthens the urethra and the urethral walls and works to create thick, plentiful semen. Some men have a problem of discharging semen when they urinate. Banyan tree milk is useful in correcting this condition as well as premature ejaculation. Take six drops a day in honey, mixed with a little yogurt, for six to eight days. For best results, abstain from sex beginning six to eight days before the treatment and continuing eight to ten days after. This regimen is best practiced in the spring or fall, early spring being best.

*Figs.* For sexual or nervous disorders, a mono diet of fresh figs important — and be sure to eat the white strings which cling to the yogurt to ten or fifteen figs is a good ratio. *Also see Golden Figs.*

*Garlic,* a "trinity root," stimulates the production of semen. It gives sexual energy which can be channeled into creativity. Any man who is married and wants to remain married should somehow manage to eat two cloves of garlic per day. Raw garlic is best, but lightly cooked is also effective. Many people find the smell of garlic odd or unpleasant, but this amazing root which makes you smell on the outside eliminates many of the bad smells inside the body. If you (or the people you work with) find the garlic smell truly offensive, it is widely available as garlic oil in capsules. *See Garlic Toast.*

*Ghee,* or clarified butter, is the oil of choice in a man's diet. According to Indian tradition, the man who regularly uses more ghee than any other oil will never have problems with his sexual world. It will not make you overweight or underweight, but it will create semen. Use as you would butter or cooking oil. *See Recipes.*

*Nutmeg* has the property of lowering the blood pressure. In a healthy male, it brings about immediate temporary impotency. However, for those who are unable to control their sexual discharge, or who have trouble with premature ejaculation, this little nut is divine. For this purpose, take 1 to 2 teaspoons of fresh ground nutmeg (not powdered) in a few ounces of yogurt just prior to intercourse. Too much nutmeg can cause dizziness and disorientation; however, eaten with banana, it is a tonic for men which can keep them young for years. *See Banana-Nutmeg Icecream.*

*Onion,* another "trinity root," also increases semen production and generates sexual energy.

*"P" fruits* — peaches, plums, pineapples, pears, papayas and persimmons — are good for a man's creativity. To these we have to add "pananas," though you may spell it with a *b.* The best way to eat these fruits is to blend them really well with yogurt, then drink as a "fruit smoothie."

*Pistachios.* A handful of pistachio nuts should be in every man's daily diet. Eat them raw, unsalted and unskinned. *See Trinity Saffron Nut Spread, Pistachio Paranthas, and Golden Fig Nut Chutney.*

*Saffron* is a concentrated heat in the form of an herb. It provides the "atomic energy" of the human life force. According to Indian scriptures, it can be used for skin problems, hair problems, old age and senility, and can add to a man's overall health and vigor. *See Saffron Almond Rice, Golden Figs, Golden Fig Nut Chutney, Pistachio Paranthas, and Trinity Saffron Nut Spread.*

# Chapter Seven:

# Foods for Women

As we said at the beginning of the last chapter, men and women are different in many ways. They require different foods and different eating habits. What a woman eats is particularly important. The majority of women's sicknesses and sexual handicaps come from eating the wrong foods. Sixty percent of their physical ailments and eighty percent of their mental ailments can be traced to bad diet. Wrong food leads to problems in sexual behavior and a negative mental attitude. There are certain foods which are especially necessary for women. These include citrus fruits, plums, peaches, papayas, raisins and dates. Women who are wives or mothers often feel obliged to eat whatever they have fixed for their husbands or children, and seldom think of their own special food needs. In this case, it is best for a woman to fix a separate portion of "her own food" and eat that instead.

The most common problem that women have with food is poor elimination. We discussed earlier the importance of eliminating whatever you eat within twenty-four hours. Actually, in the case of women, the maximum time for good health is eighteen hours. As a woman, you may eat for eating's sake or you may eat for taste, but whatever you eat, it must clear your stomach in two hours and your entire body in eighteen hours. Otherwise, you are asking for problems. So, as a general rule, a woman should build her diet around foods that are eliminated easily. Foods like watermelon, beets, beet greens, and all other green vegetables are a must. So are all sorts of seeds.

Certain foods are definitely not for women. If taken regularly, they contribute to her becoming unhealthy and losing her radiance. Alcoholic drinks and stimulating drinks like coffee, tea, and heavily sugared drinks are not women's food. Heavy acid-producing foods like meat should not be taken. Anything which produces cholesterol, like eggs or saturated fats, is very dangerous to a woman's health. Likewise, a woman should consider salt and sugar as enemies because they take away one of her finest assets, her beauty. Salt should be generally avoided because it causes water retention, to which a woman is prone anyway. Instead of salt, use lemon juice as a seasoning.

For a woman, the best pattern of eating is to have two solid meals a day plus two liquid meals. Otherwise her tendency is to eat like a goat, nibbling all the time. Breakfast should be a light, healthy thick drink made with juice or milk. (*See Ms. Whiz*) At lunchtime, you can eat as heavy a meal as you can easily digest. A second liquid meal can be taken in the midafternoon. Dinner should be very light and digestible. If you can make this mainly a vegetable meal, it will give you tremendous physical security. Steamed vegetables are good at this meal, or fresh green salads served with an oil and lemon dressing. A woman should never eat salad without dressing. Tofu (soybean cake) is also a good food to include in this meal, however it should be cooked before eating.

Women should be especially careful about fasting. Generally speaking, because of her constitutional makeup, a woman should not fast on liquids for more than a day. However, if fasting is required, she should be careful to prepare herself and to seek professional guidance. Otherwise, there is a high risk that her pulse at the navel point will go off center. This can adversely affect her breasts, her pituitary gland, and her digestive system. A woman should not go on a mono diet for more than seven to ten days unless supervised by a specialist. In some cases, a specialist may recommend a mono diet of thirty days.

# MENSTRUATION AND FOOD

A woman's menstrual cycle can be disrupted by the foods she eats. This happens when her food makes her blood overacidic. As we've seen in Chapter Two, the biggest cause of overacidity is meat in the diet. Basically, a woman is not supposed to eat meat. Meat is more harmful to her than to a man because her reproductive organs are very delicate. Unfortunately, when a woman stops eating meat, her period is likely to become irregular for a while as her body goes through a period of cleansing.

During the first five mornings of her menstrual flow, a woman should eat a handful of unpeeled almonds sauteed in ghee or almond oil as a small breakfast. A little honey should be added, not just as a sweetener, but because it increases calcium retention and rejuvenates the reproductive system. Except for during her period, or after giving birth to a child, almonds should be eaten without the peels, since they are very astringent and can detract from a woman's youth. Soak the almonds overnight in cold water. The peels can then be easily removed by hand.

*For relief from menstrual cramps* and general fatigue, ginger tea is recommended. It works directly on the lower back, glands and nerves. Boil four to five slices of peeled fresh ginger root in three cups of water. Add milk and honey to taste and drink. You can boil cardamon in with the ginger for extra flavor, or as an alternative, make *Yogi Tea* with extra ginger.

Another aid for relief of menstrual discomfort is to saute onions, garlic and ginger in raw vegetable oil or ghee until brown, then add fresh-ground black pepper, and mix with *Mung Beans and Rice*.

*For weakness due to menstruation,* take 1 to 2 tablespoons of raw sesame oil each day, beginning a few days before the onset of your period and continuing until four to five days after your period is over. It will give you energy and, taken regularly, may eliminate feelings of weakness at this time of the month altogether. *See Ms. Whiz.*

*For irregular menstrual flow,* one week before the onset of your period eat *Eggplant Pakoras.*

*For thick and long menstrual flow* and impure blood, boil black peppercorns in milk and drink. Lecithin and vitamin E are also useful supplements for this condition.

*To correct cycle irregularities,* include plenty of mangoes in the diet, or eat a simple fruit or vegetable diet. You can also boil black peppercorns in milk and take that as a mono diet for five to six days. Swallow the peppercorns whole with the milk. *See Mango Lassi.*

## HORMONAL IMBALANCE

Sometimes there is an imbalance in a woman's hormones, including her estrogen level. This can affect her behavior, making her argumentative, nagging and insecure. It is not a woman's natural behavior to be obnoxious and ungracious, but a hormonal imbalance can cause changes in her glandular system which make her act that way. The following mono diets have been found to be effective in correcting such an imbalance. Each may be practiced for five to ten days, but no longer without competent medical supervision:

*White Turnip Fast.* Steam white turnips (sometimes called "underground apples") and mash them. After mashing, add almond oil, turmeric, a pinch of salt, and pepper. It will look like a pudding. If you want, you can steam the turnip greens and eat them as well. It is very healthful.

*Daikon Radish Fast.* Eat nothing but daikon radishes, raw or steamed. It is very cleansing to the liver as well.

*Beet Green Fast.* Eat nothing but steamed beet greens for five to ten days.

## CALCIUM/MAGNESIUM IMBALANCE

This is a common problem for women. After the age of eighteen, every woman should take a complete daily supplement, like Rice Bran Syrup, which contains all the necessary minerals.

Cold-pressed sesame oil is an excellent source of calcium. *See Ms. Whiz and Sesame Yogurt Dressing.*


## MENOPAUSE

At the age of thirty-six, a woman is potentially subject to menopause, although in a perfectly healthy woman, it should not occur until age fifty-four. Many mental and physical inadequacies result from the decreased flow of estrogen, but they can be overcome through the use of Vitamin E, chlorophyll and raw vegetable oils such as sesame, coconut, peanut, olive, and (the supreme) almond oil. When a woman reaches her twenty-eighth year, she should start the habit of taking an ounce (2 tablespoons) of raw almond oil a day, either in milk or in any other way that suits her. *(See Ms. Whiz.)* When taken in its raw, cold-pressed, unsaturated form, it lowers cholesterol, reduces body fat, cleanses the body of toxins, keeps the skin healthy and lustrous, provides necessary protein, and takes away hunger. Quite a lot from just one ounce of oil! Taken before bed, it acts as a gentle laxative as well.


## FOOD AND SEXUALITY

Here are three foods that enhance a woman's sexuality:

*Eggplant.* This is the most powerful vegetable for a woman. It energizes her entire system and keeps her going. *See Eggplant Pakoras.*

*Pickled Mango.* A woman's sexuality is represented in the Indian scriptures by the pickled mango. It is one of the most powerful sexual foods for a woman. The only thing to be careful about is that the mango is an acidic fruit. If you eat too much, it can acidify your blood, and that will make your menstrual flow very long. That is why in India they say, "If you have eaten a mango, drink milk."

*Yogi Tea.* A woman should avoid stimulating drinks, but yogi tea, which is spicy and energizing, suits her very well. The recipe comes from an ancient scripture on sex for women, in which it says that before she even thinks of having sexual intercourse, a woman should have a cup of yogi tea sweetened with honey. (Her husband should have a cup after intercourse.) *See Recipes.*

## OTHER GOOD FOODS FOR WOMEN

*Fruits* of many kinds are excellent for women. Especially good are apricots, peaches, plums, persimmons, papayas, figs, pears, bananas, pomegranates, and oranges. Persimmons enhance a woman's sexual energy. Mangoes are good for menstrual disorders. They work on the entire female sexual system. *See Mango Lassi.*

*Green Chiles.* In India they say, "A woman can live without a man, but she cannot live without green chiles." Chiles are a must for women. They provide the following benefits: 1. They prevent mouth odor which comes with menstruation. 2. They prevent constipation and do not allow waste pockets to develop in the intestinal tract. 3. They provide a very concentrated dose of Vitamin C. 4. They give the body chlorophyll, which a woman needs more than any other creature on earth. *See Chiles and Cheese, Nut Curry Supreme and Jalapeno Milk.*

*Salad Dressing* is essential when a woman wants to eat raw, leafy vegetables. Eaten plain, they can create painful abdominal gas, and can also cause problems during pregnancy. (A woman should avoid any food that creates gas.) The best salad dressing is made with oil and vinegar, or oil and lemon. Use malt vinegar, not white. In the summer, olive oil is very good; in the winter, sesame oil. Make sure the oil is cold-pressed. It is best to leave the dressing on the salad for about fifteen minutes prior to serving. *See Sesame Yogurt Dressing.*

*Turmeric* is a healer for a woman's internal organs. At least 2 tablespoons per week should be incorporated into her diet. It is the most healing root for the body. It will purify a woman's blood and keep her beautiful. It is excellent for the maintenance of the mucous membranes, especially the female sexual organs. *See Golden Milk, Nut Curry Supreme and Yogurt Curry.*

*Wheatberries* (unground whole wheat) are a very nourishing and cleansing food for a woman. Set to boil in plenty of water overnight, they are an excellent food for a one-day fast every week. They will bring health to her intestinal tract, and beauty to her face and skin. They will also enhance the sense of taste, build strong gums and teeth, and prevent lower back pain. If a woman starts this routine early in life and keeps it up, menopause may pass by almost unnoticed. Boil wheatberries until soft and puffy, then serve with milk and honey.

*Yogurt.* A woman should eat plenty of "homemade" acidophilus yogurt. It is very cleansing to her digestive system. It can be used in a douche, or applied externally as a deep cleanser for the skin. *See Recipes.*

*Chapter Eight:*

# Foods for Children

Diet is the foundation for a child's entire being, physically, mentally and spiritually. Children have been found to change dramatically in their physical abilities, mental clarity and psychological balance by changing their diets. In addition, a child learns basic attitudes towards food and habits of eating in the early years. So the way you decide to feed your child is extremely important.

## BREASTFEEDING

If possible, it is best to breastfeed your child. It is a miracle that within the breast of a woman, God can turn blood into milk to feed the young. Breastmilk provides the child with all the nutrients it needs and provides natural immunization against many diseases. Breastmilk is the purest milk a child can receive and the kind most suited to the child's system. Although variation is possible, it is suggested that a child be nursed throughout the first year of life.

In addition to breastmilk, the newborn should be given ample water. Cardamon water (water boiled with cardamon seeds, then sweetened with honey) is especially good since it helps to eliminate gas from the baby's digestive tract. It is better to use a small spoon or a dropper than a bottle to serve the water, since the easy suction of the bottle may make the child "lazy" at its mother's breast.

After the first forty days, other liquid foods may be added. Fruit or vegetable juices diluted with water or whey in a ratio of 1 to 10 may be introduced. Almond milk, wheat milk and walnut milk are very healthful for children. Or you can blend a little banana into a cup of whey for a tasty drink. Introduce these new foods gradually, beginning with just a few teaspoons a day, and increasing up to about six ounces per day. Later on, you will find them very helpful in substitute feedings when your baby is being weaned. A mixture of equal parts of sesame, olive and almond oils may be given, five drops per day, as a supplement. It will help with the digestion of the wheat and nut milks listed above.

## FIRST SOLID FOODS

Sometime between the six and twelfth month, solid foods may be introduced. Usually at about the time teeth are coming in, a baby develops the digestive juices necessary to handle solid foods. The first foods to be introduced should be mashed fruits. (Until a child has molars, all solid food must be mashed or blended.) Introduce new foods slowly, feeding your child the same food for three or four days before introducing another. This will allow you to watch for allergies or digestive problems. If the child becomes unusually irritable, or breaks out in a rash after the introduction of a new food, then he may be allergic to that food. Infant allergies are usually short-lived due to their immature digestive systems, so wait and introduce the same food a few months later. Also check the child's stool to see if the new food went out as it came in. If so, then your child is not yet ready for the new food. In children as in adults, the stool should float if the food is being thoroughly digested.

Bananas or baked apples are excellent fruits to start with. Be especially sure that the bananas are not over- or underripe. Later, you can add peaches, pears, papayas and avocados. Mangoes are a good food for children, but they must be blended with milk to counteract their acidity. After fruits, you can begin to introduce cooked vegetables blended with a few drops of cold-pressed vegetable oil. Cooked carrots are often a favorite. Be sure, once again, to introduce the foods slowly, one at a time.

Between eight and twelve months, you can begin to offer your child simple dairy products like yogurt, cottage cheese and paneer. (A child is not ready for hard cheese until about three years of age.) Blended grains, nuts and seeds can also be cautiously introduced. Nuts and seeds can be served in the form of nut butters, and grains in the form of zwieback. Wheat and rice can be blended into a fine mush. In no case should children be served grains or nuts whole, as their digestive systems are not ready to cope with them.

## SETTING UP A FEEDING SCHEDULE

Setting up a feeding schedule for your child is essential, both to insure that he or she is neither overfed nor underfed, and to provide your child with an inner security about eating. Children first come to understand time through their feeding schedules. If they can be taught from an early age to expect their food on schedule, then they will develop a healthy security about eating, and will be less likely to be subject to nagging desires for food as they get older.

In setting up a schedule, you must experiment a bit at first and be sensitive to your child's needs. Some children do very well nursing every four hours, with clear liquid feedings in between. Other children must nurse every three hours, and some, especially low birth-weight or premature babies, must nurse even more often than that. Careful observation of your child will let you know what is best. Gradually, as the child gets older and can eat more during a single meal, the time between feedings can be increased.

After your child is weaned, scheduling of meals is still important. For a child of one or two, this may mean a meal or snack every two hours. For an older child, it probably means three meals a day with a snack midway between the meals. Whatever the schedule, it is important that you make the snacks into "sit-down snacks." Have the child take a break from immediate activity, sit down, and eat the snack. Then allow a few minutes before the child goes back to playing again. This promotes good digestion and good eating habits which will serve your child in years to come.

## TEETHING

Cutting teeth is a painful process. The following foods and drinks can help to accelerate the teething process and reduce pain:

*Yogi Tea* diluted with milk should be given daily. You can soak a cotton cloth with yogi tea and give it to the child to suck or chew on.

*Clove Oil.* A drop of clove oil can be applied to the gums. It may sting when first applied, but after a moment it will numb the area.

*Rice Bran Syrup.* When a child is teething, he may lose his appetite. It is important during this time to give a good vitamin supplement, both to compensate for the lack of foods and to soothe the nerves. Rice Bran Syrup is recommended. *See "Special Foods for Children" at the end of this chapter for special instructions for its use.*

*Celery Juice.* Diluted celery juice is very soothing to the child's nerves. (During this trying period, you may be wise to drink it too.) Celery juice with raisin water provides the same benefits as well as extra iron.

*Zwieback or Carrots.* Children who are teething love to chew on hard foods like zwieback or carrots. By cutting one side of the carrot in a zigzag pattern, you can make it especially nice to chew.

## GUIDELINES FOR CHILDREN'S DIETS

After weaning, a child's diet will expand rapidly. Common sense, careful observation of his eating and digestive behavior, and the following guidelines will be helpful in planning his diet:

*Feed your child only easily digestible food.* Don't serve anything which requires crunching, mashing or chewing before he has a complete set of teeth. You (or your electric blender) should do the job that baby gums cannot.

*Keep food preparation simple.* Allow your child to experience the natural taste of each food. It may taste bland and uninteresting to you, but it almost certainly does not to your child. Hot spices should not generally be introduced until age twelve, and even then in moderation.

*Serve your child the most nourishing and uncontaminated foods possible.* The food they eat during their early years is used to form their growing bodies. It is the basis of their future health. As much as possible, use fresh, unsprayed produce. Avoid canned and processed foods, and avoid preservatives. You would not knowingly build your own house with inferior materials, so don't feed your child junk!

*Do not overly sweeten your child's food, and avoid sugar.* A child's food should be just a little sweet, like the sweetness of fresh wheat bread. A child does not need an excess of sweetening; moreover, his early diet will establish his taste in food which will last a lifetime. Children who have been raised with sweeteners in moderation may experiment with commercially produced sugar candies, but rarely will they develop a "sweet tooth." Much has been written about the negative effects of sugar. We'll not discuss it here, except to recommend that you use other sweeteners, such as honey, molasses, maple syrup, or soaked dried fruits whenever possible. Although raw honey may have health benefits for older children and adults, it often contains bacteria which are upsetting to the delicate digestive system of a young child. Therefore, before the age of two, it is better to boil honey before serving it.

*Avoid salt in your child's diet.* It is not necessary, and it creates a "salt habit" which can lead to high blood pressure in adulthood. Instead, substitute mild fresh or dried herbs, kelp or vegetable salt.

*Your child needs plenty of liquids.* If the child is fussy or emotional the problem is often dehydration. Lots of liquid in the diet will help keep your child on an even keel, and will cleanse the kidneys to avoid infection. Serve liquids no sooner than twenty minutes after eating, since they may dilute the digestive juices used to process the child's meal. Juices are concentrated foods. Up until the age of three, juices should be diluted at least half and half with whey or water. Otherwise the child must produce excess acid to digest them. One glass of apple juice contains the juice of four apples, and you wouldn't serve a small child four apples!

*Serve your child a balanced diet.* Consult your doctor or a good book on nutrition if you need help. Generally speaking, though, your child's diet should consist of one-half protein foods, like cereals, nut milks and dairy, and one-half fruits and vegetables.

*Serve your child with grace.* We have already talked about the importance of eating in a pleasant relaxed environment. This principle applies to children as well as adults. If possible, don't hand your child a slice of food on the run, saying, "Here, take this." Have him sit down in a quiet spot, prepare him for his meal, and say, "May I serve you some food now?" By serving your child, you are teaching him how to serve himself.


## SPECIAL FOODS FOR CHILDREN

The following foods are especially suitable for children. Be sure, however, to read the introductory information at the beginning of this chapter to find out at what age these foods may be introduced. Some of them may not be suitable for very young children.

*Bananas* are an ideal first food to feed your child. They are high in vitamin A and potassium and, when not overripe, high in calcium. The stringy white lining of the banana peel is especially nutritious. Whey and bananas will make the child grow tall and develop good bones.

*Basmati Rice* cooked only in lemon juice helps to clean out the body after the child has been exposed to one of the normal childhood illnesses. It will help the child to build up internal resistance. Serve one-half cup every two hours with yogurt and honey.

*Celery* is one of the best foods for children. Blend up celery stalks with yogurt and honey. The beauty of celery is that it has little fibers which work like a broom to cleanse the colon.

*Chlorophyll* is useful in helping your child to digest protein. Give two or three drops in milk twice or three times daily. Chlorophyll is available in liquid form at most health food stores. As an alternative, you can serve your child one or two ounces of spinach, celery or romaine lettuce juice daily.

*Fruits* are natural foods for children. Papayas, pears, figs, peaches, oranges, baked apples . . . all are excellent. Take a good ripe peach, peel it, and give your child a free area in which to "mess around" with it! For young children, fruits are best served mashed or blended. Do not give your child undiluted fruit juices.

*Ghee* is a very pure food. If possible, it should always be substituted for butter in your family diet. (*See Recipes.*) It will combat your child's hunger. Not to be served to children directly, it can be nicely blended into steamed vegetables or *Mung Beans and Rice.*

*Grains* need to be cooked well and blended if they are to be given to children before they have molars. They must first be digested by the saliva of the mouth which is released by chewing before they enter the stomach. Wheat should not be given to very small children, except as *Wheat Milk.* Be careful not to give too many carbohydrates in your child's diet as they may upset the magnesium-phosphorus balance, causing eye, skin or mental problems.

*Kelp* is a dried seaweed. It is very strengthening and calming to your child. It is high in minerals and protein. Use as a flavoring for soups, serve as a vegetable, or granulate and sprinkle on food instead of salt.

*Milk* is very good for children, but if the cream content is more than five percent, it should be mixed with some water. Raw milk, when diluted with fifteen percent water, is a nearly perfect food. For children under three years, all cow's milk is too rich and concentrated a food and should be diluted with water.

*Mung Beans and Rice* is a very nutritious food for children (*see Recipes*) but it should be prepared without spices. Serve with a little almond oil and vegetable seasoning — no salt.

*Nut Butter.* Almonds and walnuts can be made into nut butter by blending them until they make a smooth spread. (Add a little water or almond oil so that they will blend easily.) Serve plain, with fruit, or on bread. If you feel your child should be talking but isn't, try serving nut butter with meals. It will help to exercise the small muscles in the mouth and stimulate talking.

*Paneer, or Curds* is a nutritious natural cheese. It is the only kind of cheese a young child should eat. A child's stomach digests foods very slowly and simply. Hard cheeses take too long to digest. Curds can be served alone, or with dates or honey as a sweetener. For older children, it can be sauteed in ghee. *See Paneer and Saag Paneer.* Natural cottage cheese (without any gums, gelatin or additives), which is similar to paneer, can be served when paneer is not conveniently available. As they are very concentrated forms of protein, paneer or cottage cheese should not be served to very young children.

*Peanut Oil* is very healing for a sick child, but it can't be fed to the child directly because it is difficult to digest. Instead, make dough with peanut oil, and bake it into bread. Turn that bread into zwieback, and blend the zwieback with fruit. Serve it to the child in this form.

*Steamed Vegetables* should be an important part of your child's diet from about nine months onward. For children under three, however, steamed vegetables must be blended. Be sure they are cooked properly — not to the point that they "fall apart," but not crunchy either. Serve or blend with a little ghee or raw vegetable oil. Or, for a change, boil vegetables in water and turmeric to make a soup, then blend to serve.

*Turnip.* This is a food which will make your child very bright and energetic. Steam well, then mash with a little honey. Your child will eat it like candy. (Do not serve turnip juice. It is too concentrated.)

*Whey* is a wonderful food for children. It is a clear liquid which is formed when you split milk to make paneer or curds. (*See Paneer.*) It is slightly laxative and very good for the kidneys It contains helpful bacteria which are good for the intestines. Whey is also high in minerals, and helpful in developing the long bones of the body. Whey can be mixed with apple juice for a tasty drink.

## FOODS TO AVOID

The following foods are not for children, especially young children:

*Roasted nuts or popcorn* should not be eaten until after the six-year molars have come in. Such foods, when not properly chewed, can become lodged in the digestive tract and cause severe problems.

*Soy milk* is a concentrated protein food. It is too heavy for most children, so use only under doctor's orders. (The same should apply to soy-based protein powders and soy-based infant formulas.)

*Spices*, before the age of twelve, should be avoided because they are irritating and put a pressure on the liver and kidneys. Yogi tea, however, is an exception. This special formulation is excellent for children.

*Stimulating foods*, like onions, garlic and ginger, should be limited to small quantities until the child has reached puberty. These foods generate sexual energy and are therefore inappropriate for children who have not yet reached maturity.

# RECIPES FOR CHILDREN

## ALMOND MILK
*(also Sesame, Sunflower or Walnut Milk)*
This is an excellent first food for children while they are nursing, and a great substitute for breastmilk when weaning. It is high in protein, calcium, phosphorus and iron.

*4-6 raw unsalted almonds*
*6 oz. water*
*1/2-1 tsp. cooked honey or raisins*

Soak almonds overnight in water. Peel and place in blender with a small amount of water. When blended, add remaining water, honey or raisins, and blend well. Strain through cheesecloth before serving.

For *Sesame Milk*, use a small handful of sesame seeds. For *Sunflower Milk,* use a small handful of raw, unsalted, shelled sunflower seeds. For *Walnut Milk,* use 4-6 raw, unsalted walnuts. Soak overnight and blend as above. Walnuts are good for the brain.

## APPLE MILK
This simple drink provides calcium, protein and iron in natural proportions perfect for a child. Do not serve more than 6 oz. total per day to your child. It is a good tonic for children.

*1 raw peeled apple*
*About 3 oz. milk*

Cut and blend the apple thoroughly. Then strain off the juice (use cheesecloth or a fine strainer) and mix with an equal quantity of milk.

# BAKED APPLE DELIGHT
This simple dish is always a favorite for breakfast, and it's
good for digestion too.

*1 apple*
*1 tsp. nut butter*
*4-6 oz. plain yogurt*
*1 pinch cinnamon*
*1 pinch cardamon powder*
*1/2 tsp. honey*

Bake apple until soft. Peel and remove the core. Replace core
with nut butter. Top with cinnamon, cardamon and honey. Serve
swimming in a bowl of plain yogurt. (As a slight variation, replace
honey with a moist, pitted date.)

# BANANA WHEY SMOOTHIE
If you want your children to be tall and good looking with
strong bones, feed them this simple drink. They'll grow like
bamboo shoots.

*1 ripe banana*
*4 oz. fresh fruit juice*
*4 oz. whey*
*5 drops raw almond oil*
*5 drops raw sesame oil*
*1 tsp. cooked honey (optional)*

Peel banana and slice. Scrape the white strings off the inside
of the banana peel. Place banana, strings, and all other
ingredients in the blender. Blend at medium speed. Makes 2
servings.

# BASMATI RICE SOUP

This special soup has the property of making one urinate. It is an excellent remedy for weaknesses of the urinary tract. (Adults can eat this too.)

*1 cup basmati rice*
*4 cups vegetable broth*
*1 Tbsp. honey*
*1 Tbsp. Rice Bran Syrup*

Place rice and vegetable broth in a pot and bring to a boil. (Use powdered vegetable broth if necessary, but the fresh broth from steamed vegetables is best. No oil, spices or salt!) Cover and simmer for 30 minutes. Add honey and Rice Bran Syrup. Blend well. Makes 4 servings.

# CARDAMON MILK

This drink is soothing to the digestive tract and helps a teething baby with sore teeth and gums.

*8-10 whole green cardamon pods*
*2 cups milk*
*1 tsp. vanilla extract*

Simmer cardamon pods in milk at a low temperature. Add vanilla and simmer a few minutes longer. Strain and serve.

## CELERY RAISIN DRINK
This drink will calm a child down and give him energy.

*2 stalks celery*
*1 handful raisins*

Put the celery through a juicer. Place the raisins in a pan and cover with 1 or 2 inches of springwater. Bring to a boil. Before the water boils away, remove from heat and strain raisin water into a cup. Strain celery juice and mix with raisin water. For very young children, dilute 1 to 1 with springwater.

## OASIS FRUIT SHAKE
Here's another nourishing, refreshing drink:

*1 very ripe fig*
*6 raisins*
*1 pitted date*
*1 Tbsp. cottage cheese or paneer*
*6 oz. whey*

Blend thoroughly and serve. Experiment using other fresh fruits.

## WHEAT MILK
This is a nourishing drink, and the best way to introduce your child to grains.

*1 handful wheatberries*
*8 oz. spring water*
*1/2 tsp. cooked honey*

Soak wheatberries overnight. Drain the water. Blend with springwater and honey. Strain through cheese cloth and serve.

# WHEATBERRY CREAM

Here's another way to introduce grains before a child has his molars. It tastes good too!

*1/4 cup wheatberries*
*1 cup water*
*2 Tbsp. ghee*
*2 tsp. cooked honey or maple syrup*

Put wheatberries and water in a pot. Bring to a boil and simmer for 3 hours until they are soft and puffy. Check occasionally and add water if necessary. Pour wheatberries into the blender with just enough of their own water to cover them. Blend and put through a strainer. Only the creamy part of the wheatberries should pass through; throw away the rest. Stir in honey and ghee and serve. Makes 2 servings.

# ZWIEBACK PUDDING

The best way to serve bread to a young child is in the form of zwieback. "Double baking" turns starches into sugars and makes the bread more digestible. It is best made from homemade bread, especially if you can bake it with lots of fruit and bran. (*See Fruit Bran Bread.*) However, when this is not possible, you can use a quality store-bought whole grain bread.

*1 slice homemade bread*
*1/2 cup cottage cheese*
*1/2 tsp. honey*

Place the bread in the oven and bake at 250 degrees for 2-3 hours until it forms a hard, dry toast. Break into crumbs and blend with cottage cheese and honey. Serve.

Zwieback can be served from age five or six months onward. Serve in "pudding" form, as in this recipe, or plain to help your child with teething.

# Chapter Nine:

# *Fasting*

Fasting is more than just the absence of food. It is a very powerful tool for healing and strenghtening the body. Very seldom is it recommended to fast on water only. It is a good thing to fast on water once a week, but rarely is it wise to do an extended water fast. Most of the time, it is better to go on a mono diet of those foods which possess the healing properties which the body needs. It is safer, and often more effective.

As with any tool, it's important to know the proper use of fasting before starting it. Don't just go on a fast indiscriminately, because you can actually do yourself more harm than good. You should prepare yourself for the fast and make sure you have the capacity to go through with it. Preparing for a fast begins with modifying your diet. Eliminate junk foods or nonfoods, and begin eating lighter meals composed mostly of vegetables or fruits. Then try fasting for a meal or too, then for a whole day. When you feel comfortable with light eating and occasional one-day fasting, then you're probably ready to try a fast of three to five days. It is always best to be under the supervision of a health practitioner, especially on your first fast, or any time you fast for more than seven to ten days. The key words are preparation, moderation and supervision.

Although anytime is appropriate for starting a fast, springtime is best. The exact time of spring varies from region to region, but it is the time when the climate is changing from cold to warm and nature is reawakening. In the body, it is the time when the blood starts changing. This makes it a perfect time to cleanse and rebuild the system. The other time it is important to start a fast is when you need to heal a particular ailment. Again, this is best done under the guidance of an experienced health practitioner.

People who fast for the first time are often surprised to find that sticking to their diets is only half the challenge of fasting. Often the physical cleansing of a fast is accompanied by a mental cleansing as well. The discipline of the fast can bring out a lot of anger and negativity. If a person has used eating to quell emotional appetites, then a fast may uncover these unfulfilled needs as well. The best way to deal with inner cleansing is just to stand back and let it happen. Try to view your negativity impartially as an observer. Every negative thought has a positive thought as its hidden twin. Simply watching a negative thought may cause its positive twin to appear. Then, by substituting the positive thought for the negative, you can change your consciousness from minus to plus.

How you break a fast is very important. Fasting cleanses the body, but is also makes it very sensitive. If you eat nothing but steamed greens for a month and then break your fast with a pizza and a soda, your body is likely to have some rather unpleasant things to say to you! It's become unused to handling heavy foods and stimulants. For this reason, you should break a fast slowly. Begin with lemon water and honey, or with fruit. Then gradually add light dairy products or vegetables. Save the more slow-to-digest foods — nuts, grains and hard cheese — for last.

One more word of warning. If you've been eating junk food for a long time, or in other ways abusing your body, don't expect to entirely cleanse your system overnight. Go slowly and steadily, making modest dietary changes at first. You will see gradual improvements. Once you have effectively cleansed your system, don't expect to go back on junk foods without paying for it. Your body, having become accustomed to a higher grade fuel, will not tolerate the heavy stimulants and nonfoods you once loved. Go back to eating junk foods if you like, but be prepared for your body to protest.


## REJUVENATING DIET

If you are eager to bring about a distinct improvement in your general health, a good first diet is to eat only fruits, nuts and vegetables (cooked or raw) for thirty days. This diet is used in India when a person is feeling old and the body is wearing out. It cleanses and revitalizes the body.

During the first few days, you may feel weak, but gradually your strength will increase and you will start to feel light and happy. After thirty days, you can continue the diet, but milk products can also be eaten. The best time for this fast is when the weather is warm and fruits and vegetables are in season.


## MUCUSLESS DIET

This is a good beginner's diet. It eliminates toxins and reduces the level of mucus in the body. It is a good basic diet to go on after you've had a cold. Try it for a week.

Eat fruits, nuts or steamed vegetables. Allow four hours between meals. Drink fresh fruit juices with the pulp left in. Add a little black pepper to the juice to aid in the elimination of intestinal gas.

During the first four days, you may feel weak. During this time, foot massage with almond oil can be very soothing. After the fourth day, strength will gradually return. Get lots of exercise during the last days of this diet. It is best to avoid sex during this rejuvenating period.


## GREEN DIET

This is a rebuilding diet. It is used to alkalinize the body, lose weight, clear the skin and cleanse the liver. It is also useful in relieving a toxic mucus condition.

76

For forty days, eat only green foods. That means salads, steamed greens, avocados, sprouts, green olives and mung beans. Unless you are using this diet to correct acne, green fruits such as honeydew, green apples and green grapes can be included. Yogi tea can be taken throughout this fast. Once a week, if you feel that you need more protein, you can eat a handful of nuts and a portion of cooked grains, but don't overdo it! By eating too many nuts and grains you'll give yourself a stomach ache and defeat the purpose of your fast.

When you break the fast, first add fruits, then grains, and finally dairy.

# FRUIT FAST

When the spring comes, it is wonderful to go on a fruit diet. Do it during April or May for one month. Just say to yourself, "I am going to eat only fruits and nothing else." Eat only one kind of fruit at a time. If you mix fruits in the same meal, you can mess up your whole system. Also, don't drink fruit juices on this fast. They are a concentrated food. Only eat whole fruit. This is an especially good diet for men.

# MUNG BEANS AND RICE

This is a good cleansing diet which still gives you plenty of nourishment if you have to work hard. It is a good winter fast, and it is especially recommended for people over forty. Mung Beans and Rice is good for the kidneys, colon and digestive organs. It is also beneficial in cases of constipation, or when food is not being digested thoroughly by the intestines. Mung beans are a very easily assimilated form of protein. Combined with rice and cooked until they have a soupy consistency, they are really a "predigested" food. *(See Mung Beans and Rice.)*

For thirty days, eat only mung beans and rice at mealtimes, with lots of fresh vegetables cooked into the same dish. Fruit may be eaten between meals as a snack, and you can drink yogi tea. As a variation, you can eat mung beans and rice with yogurt. In the winter, you can grind chiles into it to make it hot and spicy.

You can live on this diet alone for years and years and be very healthy. In India, there was a very saintly person. Mung beans and rice with yogurt was his entire diet. He would make it each night and eat it for breakfast the next morning. That man was a radiant light, just from the food he ate. People would come from all over to be healed by this man. Each morning they would form a long line outside his door. Whatever sickness they had, he would give them mung beans and rice with yogurt. And they would be cured! That's why it is called the food of angels. It has protein, carbohydrates, everything you need.

*78*

## MELON DIET

When the weather is hot, there is a fast you can do which will clean the liver, kidneys and intestines, renew the body fluids, and help you lose weight. You will need an ample supply of papayas, cantaloupes, watermelons and lemons. Here's how it works:

*Days 1 to 3.* Eat only cantaloupes. They are warming and laxative.

*Days 4 to 6.* Eat only watermelons. They are cooling to the body, and they will work on the liver and kidneys.

*Days 7 to 9.* Eat only papayas. They will work on the intestines and digestion.

*Days 10 to 12.* Drink lemon and honey dissolved in water. It rids the system of excess mucus. Do not eat any solid food.

*Days 13 to 15.* Drink only plain water. Don't drink it ice cold.

*Days 16 to 18.* Reverse the process! Drink lemon-honey water and nothing else.

*Days 19 to 21.* Eat only papayas.

*Days 22 to 24.* Eat only watermelons.

*Days 25 to 27.* Eat only cantaloupes.

To break this fast, eat only fruit at first. Then add yogurt if desired, then vegetables. Break this fast very slowly and cautiously. Do not eat nuts and grains right away or you'll suffer. It is advisable, during this fast, to massage the whole body frequently with almond oil.

This is a fairly strenuous fast. It can be modified by reducing each of the three central stages — days 10-12, 13-15 and 16-18 — to one day each, making the diet last a total of twenty-one days. This makes the fast a little easier, but it still should not be attempted by someone with little experience with fasting. This diet has very beautiful effects, but your body must first be prepared.


## BANANA FAST

This is another fast which is best not attempted by people with little experience of fasting. However, it has some very beautiful and unique effects. For those who have a history of drug abuse, it removes drug deposits from the medulla. It also rebuilds worn tissues and adjusts the iron, sodium and calcium factors in the body by replacing sodium with calcium.

*For breakfast:* Drink 1 cup of fresh-squeezed orange juice with the pulp left in it, sweetened with honey. After one hour, eat 3 medium-size ripe bananas. Chew thoroughly — this is very important — and be sure to eat the white strings which cling to the peels. Immediately after eating the bananas, eat the seeds from one whole cardamon pod. The cardamon liquifies the banana and makes it easier to digest.

*For lunch:* Eat 3 bananas followed by the seeds of 1 cardamon pod.

*For dinner:* Eat 3 bananas followed by the seeds of 1 cardamon pod.

Begin on the new moon and continue for fourteen days until the full moon. Yogi tea may be taken along with this fast.

This fast may have its side effects, so be prepared! You may feel weak from the lack of customary nervous stimulants. In that case, drink more orange juice with honey during the day. If you become constipated, increase your intake of cardamon to a maximum of three pods at a time. Also, drink large amounts of hot water regularly. People often report that this diet makes them feel more emotional and hot-tempered. If you can stay with it, it will help to balance your emotions. If you experience a severe reaction to the fast, discontinue it according to the procedure below.

*Breaking the fast:* On the fifteenth day of the moon, drink only lemon juice in warm water with honey and eat no solid food.

*Follow-up diet:* To rebuild the body after this fast, eat mung beans and rice for twenty-eight days. You can also eat fruit and yogi tea, but no dairy. The recipe for mung beans and rice must be altered slightly for this diet. Follow the recipe in the back of this book, but make the following changes:

*Use 2 cups basmati rice*
*Use 10 cups water*
*Add 1 Tbsp. fresh or dried mint leaves*
*Instead of "assorted vegetables" use green vegetables only.*

## JUICE FASTS

Should one ever go on a juice fast? Yes, but only with extreme caution and wisdom. Juice fasting is good, but it does not take care of the intestinal tract. Toxins are released very rapidly, but there is nothing in the juice to form a stool, so the toxins may not be properly eliminated, causing severe problems. The rapid release of toxins in itself may be too strong for some people, causing extreme fatigue, weakness and malaise.

On the positive side, fasting on juices increases the cleansing capacity of the lungs, liver, kidneys, bowels and skin. It rejuvenates the mental, glandular, hormonal and nervous systems. It can also help to expel decaying cells and stimulate the growth of new ones. Drinking raw vegetable juices is the easiest way to ingest high percentages of the vitamins and minerals contained in these foods.

The best juices for fasting are alkaline juices. Those often recommended include carrot, beet and carrot, celery or a combination of the three. Beet juice is very powerful and should not be taken alone. Cabbage, parsley and cucumber juices are also used therapeutically. The nutrients in fresh vegetable juices are assimilated in a matter of minutes, but in order to be properly digested they must be "chewed," thoroughly mixed with saliva, before swallowing. *Specific recommendations for juice fasts and juice supplements can be found in Chapter Ten.*

## Chapter Ten:

# Body Systems &
# Their Ailments

### AGING

There is no cure for growing older, but with proper care of the body and a positive attitude towards life, it is possible to grow older while maintaining a youthful body and spirit. Aside from regularly following the guidelines set out in earlier chapters, the following foods, when added to your regular diet, will help to maintain youthfulness.

**To maintain youthfulness.** *Datemilk* is a good energy food which helps to maintain youthfulness. A pudding made from flaxseed will balance the metals in the body and clear the digestive tract. Eaten regularly, it will keep you feeling young. One ounce of sesame oil with 6 ounces of milk daily will help to preserve youthfulness. *Also see Banana Nutmeg Icecream.*

**For a youthful appearance.** One glass of cucumber juice every morning helps to maintain a youthful appearance. Rosehips are an excellent aid for health and beauty. They provide vitamin C and bioflavinoids which support the collagen in the body. For this reason, they help keep the skin beautiful, preventing wrinkles, flabbiness and discoloration. Rosehips also have a stimulating, rejuvenating effect on the glands.

**For rejuvenation.** Whey is very helpful in the digestion and elimination of food. It inhibits the growth of harmful bacteria in the intestines by supporting the growth of helpful bacteria. It helps prevent constipation, and is high in B vitamins. As a tonic for rejuvenation, take 5 grams of vitamin C in 12 ounces of whey three times a day. *To make whey, see recipe for Paneer. Also see "Rejuvenating Diet" — Chapter Nine.*

**Retirement diet.** Around the age of fifty, a person's diet should change. The body must be treated more carefully so that the latter years can be lived without pain and suffering. If they have not already been eliminated, meat, fish, poultry and eggs should be removed from the diet at this time. Ghee, butter and rich desserts should be reduced to a minimum. A larger portion of the diet should be made up of fresh fruits and vegetables. Such a diet not only takes pressure off the body, it frees the mind and spirit. For those who would like to spend their retirement years in peace and contentment, this diet is a great help.

## THE BLOOD

**For cleansing and purifying the blood,** the following foods have been found to be helpful: A diet of baked apple and cottage cheese cleanses and renews the entire blood content. Oranges and lemons are good blood purifiers. They stir up acids and mucus for elimination. Garlic has been called a natural antibiotic. Most effective when eaten raw, it purifies the blood by drawing poisons to itself. Raw onion will attack almost anything which adversely affects the blood, but don't eat it if you have ulcers or high blood pressure. Grapes are good blood purifiers and body builders. They have been used as a mono diet to completely transform the blood in the case of certain chronic illnesses. Parsley is high in minerals and useful for building the blood. Freshly ground black pepper, tofu, turmeric and curry with unpolished rice, and sarsaparilla are also effective for blood purification. *See Old Fashioned Root Beer and Yogurt Curry.*

**For blood toxicity,** a rice dish made with the broth of onion, garlic and ginger is the best food to speed a person's recovery. (*See Trinity Rice.*)

**For anemia.** The following foods are known to increase the iron content of the blood: *Almond Milk (see children's recipes — Chapter Eight)*; seeds, such as apricot kernels, watermelon seeds, zucchini seeds and sunflower seeds (*see Nut Curry Supreme*); tofu; and mungbean sprouts. For a tasty way to get your iron, make a sandwich with tofu, tomato, onions and mungbean sprouts. Eat as many as you like!

## THE BRAIN

The brain needs carbohydrates to function properly. Carbohydrates turn into glucose which is fuel for the brain. They are essential, even if you are hypoglycemic. A prolonged carbohydrate-free diet can adversely affect thought processes. Brain foods include bread, corn, rice, seeds, oranges, olives, onions, tomatoes, walnuts and the herb *gotu kola*. Gotu kola helps keep the endocrine and sex glands in peak condition and also energizes nerve and brain functions. Chinese vegetarians who took ginseng and gotu kola every day were reported to have lived for more than two hundred years with the bodies of fifty-year-olds.

**To remove mental and sexual fatigue,** go on a diet of tomato and mint. Use 5-10 young, large, perfect fresh tomatoes. Put them in hot water just long enough so you can peel the skins off easily. (Avoid the skin because it doesn't digest.) When you have peeled the tomatoes, sprinkle with crushed dried mint leaves and soy sauce to taste. Eat three times a day for one week. You'll become a new person, clear and conscious. *Also see Parsley Pilau and Nut Curry Supreme.*

**To remove drug deposits from the medulla,** *see "Banana Fast" — Chapter Nine.*

## CARDIOVASCULAR SYSTEM

**For a healthy heart.** In India they say that if you eat celery hearts, you need never fear a heart attack. *Also see Dried Honey Apples.*

**For high blood pressure,** the following foods may be of help: Seaweed, such as kelp, contains iodine which helps keep blood pressure down. Melons are a cooling food which help to lower high blood pressure. Buckwheat contains rutin which is good for reducing blood pressure. Garlic, nutmeg and watercress are also useful in reducing blood pressure. Nutmeg can cause dizziness and disorientation. For a safe way to take nutmeg, *see Banana-Nutmeg Icecream.*

**Other beneficial foods.** Chiles stimulate blood circulation. Ginseng is good for the heart and circulatory system. You can take up to fifteen drops of extract in a glass of water four times per day. Lecithin has an affinity to oil. It combines with free fats in the bloodstream and along arterial walls. It thus promotes circulation, reduces high blood pressure, and helps to prevent heart attacks. Lemon juice thins the blood and promotes circulation.

## COLDS, INFECTIONS & FEVER

**To avoid colds,** one day a week you should fast on warm water only. This will help keep the bowels working properly and avoid a buildup of waste matter in the colon which is an indirect cause of colds. Yogi tea, taken regularly, also helps prevent colds.

**Good foods for colds and flu:** Quinine comes from the cinchona tree. It is a natural medicine which can be taken when you feel a cold or flu coming on. Take one 5-grain capsule with 8 ounces of milk. Or, take one 5-grain capsule with 10 ounces of milk and 3 tablespoons of cold-pressed olive oil. During the flu season, you may try taking 9 ounces of warm milk with 4 tablespoons of cold-pressed olive oil before bed each night, plus one 5-grain quinine capsule before bed and one in the morning. It is a very effective precautionary measure. *Always* take quinine with milk.

*Yogi Tea* is good for any kind of respiratory or sinus cold. In some cases, a three-day fast on yogi tea is recommended. Yogi tea has been successfully used during epidemics of influenza as a preventive measure. Persons drinking Yogi Tea in place of all other liquids proved effectively resistant to the disease.

Watermelon juice may be taken instead of a meal if you think you are getting a cold. It cleans and regulates the liver, causes the kidneys to secrete, inhibits mucus formation, and reduces swelling of the mucous membranes.

One more good remedy when you feel a cold or flu coming on is *Jalapeno Milk.*

**To guard against viral infections,** serve your family *Saffron Almond Rice* (with seeds) once every month. It is really delicious, and it will increase their resistance to viruses.

**For chest colds,** apply eucalyptus externally on the throat and chest.

**Fever** is the body's natural defense against poisons, viruses and other stress factors. The high temperatures speed the metabolism, increase blood circulation, and inhibit the growth of viruses and bacteria. Unless the fever becomes dangerously high (in which case, consult your doctor), the best thing you can do is to let it be. However, the following recommendations may help to ease the discomfort of fever and speed recovery.

**For achiness and discomfort of fever,** use ginger tea, which is very soothing to the nervous system. Ginger tea is made by boiling 4 or 5 slices of fresh ginger root in 3 cups of water. Add honey to taste. Foot massage is also very soothing to the nervous system and stimulating to all the internal organs. It will help a person relax. For best results, massage in a mixture of almond oil and onion juice.

**To break a fever,** serve the patient *Spiced Chapatis.* They will make him sweat and break the fever. Good for both children and adults.

**For recovery from fever or smallpox,** drink *Datemilk.* It is a quick source of energy and a very nourishing food.

## EARS
Listening is the most important human faculty. Therefore the ears should be given the best care.

**To eliminate excess ear wax,** strain onion juice and warm it by dipping a spoon in boiling water and then filling the spoon with onion juice. Pour into the ears, then plug with cotton overnight.

**For earaches,** fry an onion in vegetable oil. When the oil has cooled so that it is just barely warm, place a few drops of the oil in the affected ear. If the condition persists, see a doctor.

# EYES

**To prevent eye diseases,** first thing in the morning splash cold water into the open eyes. Or, when brushing your teeth in the morning, begin by "brushing" the back of the throat. This will make you gag slightly, and will bring up mucus. It will also make the eyes tear, washing the surfaces of the eyes.

**To keep the eyes healthy,** drink a mixture of 6 ounces of carrot juice, 6 ounces of celery juice, 2 ounces of endive juice and 2 ounces of parsley juice. Almonds are also good for the eyes. *See Nut Curry Supreme.*

**For poor eyesight,** a diet of eight pounds of mangoes and a half gallon of milk per day may be helpful.

**For soreness and redness,** place grated raw potato between two pieces of sterile gauze and apply to the eyes. When the potato dries out, replace it.

**For bloodshot eyes,** apply a drop of warm honey to the open eyes.

# GALLBLADDER

**To cleanse the gallbladder,** horseradish is an ideal food.

**For gallstones,** drink the following mixture: 6 ounces of carrot juice, 6 ounces of celery juice, and 4 ounces of cucumber juice.

# HABITUATION

All problems of addiction and negative habit formation have both a physical and a mental basis. The best form of treatment combines rigorous physical cleansing through special diet, exercise and breathing techniques, and the changing of mental habit patterns through meditation and positive environment. A certified facility for the holistic treatment of substance abuse is the 3HO Drug Treatment Center in Tucson, Arizona. They are very experienced and have a remarkably high success rate. They are government certified and are covered by most forms of medical insurance. Write to them directly, or ask your health practitioner. In addition, your holistic health practitioner or Kundalini Yoga instructor may be able to work with you in correcting any damage to mind or body caused by drug or alcohol abuse. See Appendix B, "3HO Healing Network," for a list of addresses. If you are suffering from an addiction, get experienced help. We have not attempted to describe a complete program of treatment in these pages. However, some of the following recommendations may be of supplemental use.

**For alcoholism,** to speed detoxification, drink lots of fresh grapefruit juice. Drink a mixture of carrot and celery juice every two hours. Alternate ratios of 3 to 1 and 1 to 3 carrot to celery juice. For three days, eat nothing but steamed beets sprinkled with brewers yeast. Eat even if you're not hungry.

**For drunkenness,** drink a blend of homemade yogurt, lemon juice and ice, then go to sleep. In the morning you will feel much better.

**Drug "freak-outs."** For a person who is freaking out on drugs, who is very agitated or very scared, the best thing to do is to massage his feet with a mixture of garlic juice and almond oil. If these are unavailable, simple foot massage may help. If necessary, call emergency medical help.

**For drug convulsions,** drink a cup of onion juice every hour as necessary.

To repair damage to nerve centers caused by drug abuse, drink *Golden Milk* every day for forty days. Yogi tea, taken regularly, helps to correct the damage done by drug use. It is especially useful in alleviating periodic depression and discouragement which may persist after drug use has stopped. Your holistic health professional or local yoga instructor may be able to prescribe special exercises to correct any damage due to drugs. *See Appendix B.*

For lethargy due to drug addiction. People who have no energy because they are on "downers" or other drugs may find that pineapple juice is a good natural source of energy.

For nicotine addiction. One way to help yourself stop smoking is to practice a breathing exercise called *Vatskar Kriya.* See your holistic health professional or Kundalini Yoga instructor. *(See Appendix B.)* You may also find it helpful to eat a pack of raisins each day. They'll give you energy and satisfy oral cravings.

## HAIR

Hair is the antenna of the body. It is the most potent and purest form of protein in the world. The roots have oil rich in protein and that oil supports the brain activity. That is why we have our longest hair on the scalp. Cutting the hair is not advisable, as the hair on the legs and armpits has a purpose too. When it is shaved, the lower spine and pituitary gland are adversely affected.

Considering all this, it is very important to take good care of your hair. Ideally, it should be combed twice daily with a *wooden comb.* If you brush your hair, then use a natural bristle brush. (Plastic generates static electricity which interferes with the subtle electrical activity of the higher centers of the brain.) Actually, it is best to keep the hair tied in a bun on top of the head, and then cover it with a cotton cloth. This provides the maximum energy to the higher centers, and insulates and protects the hair from the external environment. It also reduces split ends. By wearing it this way, you'll feel more centered and ready to face the day. At night, the hair should be brushed down and braided to prevent tangles.

**Dandruff** is treated in India by massaging a mixture of yogurt and ground sulfur into the scalp. Leave it on for a half hour to an hour and then shampoo it out. Apply weekly for four weeks.

**Also good for the hair** are chlorophyll and lecithin. Lecithin rejuvenates the hair and increases growth. Chlorophyll is high in essential fatty acids. Olive oil and almond oil applied externally are good for the hair.


## HYPOGLYCEMIA

It isn't only by drinking wine that one becomes intoxicated. When you eat chocolate cake, your blood sugar shoots up and you go into a stupor for two to three days! In America, nearly everyone is hypoglycemic. You were served so much candy as a child that your pancreas got into the habit of over-reacting. When you eat sweets, your blood sugar goes way up and then it goes way down and your mind and body become totally fatigued. Here's the problem. If you are hypoglycemic, you are supposed to eat every two hours. That takes care of your blood sugar, but you start gaining weight. What can you do?

Two foods which can help if you have hypoglycemia are buckwheat and *Mung Beans and Rice*. They are not overly fattening. They are easy to digest, and they can be eaten every four hours (in small quantities) Buckwheat is a complex carbohydrate which is metabolized very slowly and evenly. Mung beans and rice, when taken with a little yogurt, have a similar effect. You can also carry around some celery stalks and eat a few every two hours.

## INTESTINAL TRACT

**For cleansing the intestinal tract,** try beets and beet greens. The "Melon Diet" (*see Chapter Nine*) is specifically designed to clean out the intestinal tract. To cleanse the colon, "overeat" on nothing but steamed celery for twenty-four hours. Garlic neutralizes unwanted bacteria in the colon and small intestine. Oranges and lemons will stimulate intestinal peristalsis, causing hardened waste on the intestinal walls to be eliminated. *Also see Beet-Carrot Casserole, Nut Curry Supreme and Yogi Mush.*

**For intestinal gas,** eat ground black pepper on your food. Sprinkled on melons, it prevents the formation of gas. For gas in children, give them cardamon tea, made with 4-5 cardamon seeds boiled in water.

**For intestinal worms,** the following foods have been prescribed: 1 tablespoon of freshly ground coconut, followed three hours later by 1 tablespoon of castor oil, repeated daily until the cure is complete; also, the milky juice of papaya.

**To help prevent cancer of the intestinal tract or anus,** eat boiled wheatberries one day per week.

**To prevent or relieve constipation,** the following foods are recommended: 2 or 3 baked apples just before going to sleep, 2 ounces of raw almond oil taken before bed, steamed vegetables with ground black pepper, wheat bran, coconut, date skins, grapes, green chiles, a mono diet of 8 to 10 large mangoes and 8 cups of milk per day, melons, papaya, boiled onions, orange peels sauteed in turmeric, steamed mashed beets sprinkled with turmeric, and rye, which can be prepared in the form of sourdough bread.

**For acute constipation,** drink psyllium seeds in a cup of hot milk at bedtime. By four in the morning, you'll be in the bathroom. Psyllium seeds swell up to several times their size on contact with liquid, so be sure to swallow them quickly! When they swell in your intestinal tract, they take everything else with them. They are also very good for bad breath caused by digestive disorders. Senna herb tea is also a powerful laxative. (Be careful not to drink too much.)

**For chronic constipation,** a diet of cooked potatoes, potato peel broth and lots of water can be helpful. Add to this basic diet cantaloupe and steamed greens such as chard, zucchini, celery, beet tops, and turnip tops. This diet is also helpful for intestinal toxemia, uric acid disorders such as gout, and rheumatism.

**For diarrhea or dysentery.** Whenever possible, avoid diarrhea medicines such as those sold in pharmacies. They interfere with the normal functioning of the bowels which can take a very long time to become regular again. Try one of the following food remedies first. If the condition becomes severe, or if the patient becomes very weak, consult a doctor. Generally speaking, a person with severe diarrhea or dysentery should be encouraged to eat and drink regularly to avoid dehydration.

**For dysentery.** When you travel to a foreign country, there is a chance that you will get dysentery. As a preventive measure, for two weeks before you go abroad, eat a chopped raw onion in a cup of yogurt each day. The yogurt will draw the hotness out of the onion and make it taste sweet.

Peeled and grated raw apples are often effective for dysentery. Take as a mono diet for two days. On the third day, eat well-cooked *Mung Beans and Rice* with a little ghee. Eight ounces of mint tea with 2 ounces of onion juice can also give relief from dysentery, as can dates.

**Amoebic dysentery.** If dysentery persists, it may be wise to have yourself tested for amoebic dysentery. This type is caused by an amoeba which lives in the raw green vegetables of some countries. It is a more stubborn form of dysentery which should be treated by a doctor.

**For diarrhea,** try eating one banana every three hours while the condition persists. Or, take 8 ounces of mint tea with 1 ounce of onion juice every hour.

**For hemorrhoids,** try the following: Dissolve a few drops of eucalyptus oil in warm water and apply externally. In cases where hemorrhoids are a symptom of liver dysfunction, go on a mono diet of beets and beet greens or else steamed beet greens with lemon juice sprinkled on top. Hemorrhoids may appear when you are doing a cleansing fast, either as a temporary symptom, or as a sign that you are eliminating toxins faster than your system can handle them. In such cases, a diet of steamed corn for a few days may be of help. Long green chiles (not the small hot chiles), may be useful for hemorrhoids. If symptoms persist, consult your health professional.

**For colitis,** try eating chopped raw onion with yogurt.

**For irritation of the colon,** eat three ripe bananas followed by the seeds of a cardamon pod.

**To prevent waste pockets in the intestinal tract,** green chiles are recommended.

**A prolapsed transverse colon** is often a sign of lack of calcium in this area. Drink acidophilus or eat homemade acidophilus yogurt. Two tablespoons of cold-pressed sesame oil taken daily may be of help. Also try fresh coconut juice.

**Autotoxemia** due to putrefaction of waste in the colon can be prevented by eating homemade yogurt or kefir. These foods foster the growth in the intestines of "friendly bacteria" which aid in digestion, and which destroy harmful bacteria resulting from putrefaction. Yogurt can be taken orally, or used as an enema.

# LIVER
The liver performs the great service of removing toxins from the bloodstream. But if the liver becomes overtaxed to the extent that it can no longer function properly, then your whole body will

be in difficulty. Therefore, care of the liver is one of the most important aspects of preventive medicine.

**To prevent liver problems,** avoid all of the following: heavy foods, half-cooked foods, foods which take longer than twenty-four hours to digest, greasy foods, meat, fish, eggs, fried cereals, chemicals, animal fat, alcohol, and stimulating drinks like coffee which quicken digestion. Avoid eating within two hours of bedtime. If you must eat after sunset, eat only light foods, eat only until half full, and don't drink liquids with that meal. Avoid eating meals less than four hours apart, and avoid nibbling between meals.

**To cleanse the liver.** Normally, every three months you should devote at least one week to cleaning your liver. It is like changing your oil filter. The only way to do this is through diet. The following methods are effective: 1. Eat beets and beet greens, beets and carrots, or beets, carrots and onions. *(See Beet-Carrot Casserole.)* 2. Drink beet and carrot juice. Start with 14 ounces of carrot juice to 2 ounces of beet juice. Slowly increase the proportion of beet to carrot juice up to 50-50, but no higher! Straight beet juice has much too harsh an effect on the liver. 3. Go on a mono diet of watermelons, or the Melon Diet *(See Chapter Nine.)* 4. For one week, begin each day with a glass of diluted daikon radish juice. Eat nothing but fresh, unrefrigerated yogurt, and drink watermelon juice with a little salt and pepper. During this week, do a lot of exercise which makes you sweat. If your urine turns reddish, it's a sign that your liver is in bad shape and you should go on a simple, pure diet for an extended period of time. 5. For forty days, go on a diet of steamed greens with yogurt or cottage cheese. 6. Drink daikon and carrot juice, in the ratio of 1 to 3. Or go on a diet of carrot juice and steamed daikons with ghee and black pepper.

**Also helpful in cleansing the liver** are fresh steamed artichokes, mangoes, red radishes, horseradish and oranges.

**For an enlarged liver,** go on a diet of beet greens and nothing else (only under the supervision of a health professional).

**For a heavy liver.** Sometimes your blood circulation may become poor and your liver may become very heavy, causing you to break out in pimples. In such cases, fast on daikon radishes and daikon radish greens.

**For jaundice,** the following foods may be of benefit: 1. Drink acidophilus or eat homemade acidophilus yogurt. 2. Eat well-steamed beets, beet greens and daikon radish. 3. An ancient remedy for jaundice is to take a daikon radish and cut it in quarters length-wise. Hang it outside overnight. In the morning, juice it and drink it. The result is amazing!

## NERVOUS SYSTEM

**For a weak nervous system,** yogic therapy prescribes foot massage with a mixture of garlic juice and almond oil.

**For nervousness and insomnia,** try a glass of warm milk with a little honey in it. The warmth draws blood to the stomach to quicken digestion and release tension in the abdominal area, and the milk's calcium calms the nerves. A glass of celery juice before bed will completely relax you. Also, bran tea (tea made from boiled bran) is good for nervousness.

**For people who fight constantly,** 24 ounces of cucumber juice per day will help keep them cool.

**Other good foods for the nerves include:** ginger, olives, wheatberries, bananas, yogi tea and lecithin. *See Celery Pan-*

*cakes, Sesame-Ginger Milk, Trinity Saffron Nut Spread, Yogurt Curry and Yogi Tea.*

## NOSE

**To eliminate the cause of frequent nose-bleeds,** three methods were known to the ancients. First, drink acidophilus or homemade acidophilus yogurt. Second, mix one part eucalyptus oil with nine parts almond oil. Drop into the nose, bend all the way back, then blow it out. Third, take 5 drops of sandalwood oil, 15 drops of honey and a little powdered ginger and drop it into the nose.

## OVERWEIGHT

As a person becomes older, it is natural to gain weight. The body begins retaining water and the metabolism slows down. To stay healthy, however, it is important to watch your weight. As a rule, however much you weighed when you were eighteen years old, that is the ideal weight you should strive to maintain. To do so you need to get plenty of exercise and watch your diet. If you are having trouble keeping your weight down, the following foods and diets may help.

**Reducing diets:** 1. A mono diet of raw vegetables. 2. A mono diet of any one green vegetable, steamed. (Steamed broccoli with lemon juice is often used.) 3. A mono diet of *Yogi Mush.* 4. The "Green Diet" (*see Chapter Nine*). 5. A mono diet of beets and beet greens. 6. Four slices of dry toast a day for several days. 7. A mono diet of zucchinis. 8. A diet of basmati rice cooked with lemon juice and turmeric. 9. Make a sandwich with one slice of tofu, onion, tomato and mung bean sprouts. Have as many sandwiches as you like, but only once a day. The rest of the time, drink clear liquids.

**Weight-loss foods:** *See Weight-Loss Tea and Ms. Whiz.*


## RESPIRATORY SYSTEM

**For sinus problems.** If you regularly sleep with your mouth open, it may be that your sinuses are not working properly. To clean then, put a little water in your cupped palm and inhale it into each nostril in turn. Then blow it out. Practice each night before bed.

**For hayfever,** relaxation is ultimately important. Eat a low-mucus diet (cut down on grains and dairy), and at least once a day drink black peppercorn tea. Boil 1/2 teaspoon of peppercorns per cup of water for about 5 minutes. Add honey to taste and drink. Then cover yourself with a blanket and rest for one hour. It will make you sweat. Afterwards, you will feel better.

**For fatigue due to smog,** eat *Anti-Smog Pancakes.*


## SKELETO-MUSCULAR SYSTEM

**For stiff joints,** drink *Golden Milk.* It can be of great help. It lubricates the entire system. It is very helpful to students of meditation who spend a long time sitting in cross-legged positions.

**For swollen joints,** drink potato juice and also potato peel soup.

**For arthritis,** it has proven effective in some cases to drink peppercorn tea (tea brewed from black peppercorns). This tea will make you sweat. Wrap yourself in a warm blanket, which will make you sweat even more. Practice for one hour per day. This sweating will cause you to eliminate toxins which are the cause of some forms of arthritis. *Also see Pistachio Paranthas and Old-Fashioned Root Beer.*

**Other beneficial foods.** Coconuts are good for the bones and teeth, containing many body-building minerals. Ginger root works directly on the fourth vertebra and lower back. It relieves backache, especially when caused by sexual excess. *Yogurt Curry* is very good for muscle development. *Yogi Tea* contains cinnamon, which is good for the bones.

## SKIN

Healthy skin reflects a healthy gut. The source of most skin problems is not the skin itself, but the digestive tract. So, to properly care for the skin, we must combine internal and external treatments.

**External skin preparations.** Mustard oil is a natural skin cleanser. It drains toxins from the pores and is very healing. Olive oil is very good when applied to the skin. In India, the leaves of the *neem* tree are taken as a tea for the benefit of the skin. In this country, you can find beauty soaps which contain neem oil.

**For the face,** make *Homemade Yogurt*, then churn it slowly. This will remove the butter. Take the remaining liquid and pass it through cheesecloth. What passes through the cheesecloth can be served to children to promote growth. What remains behind is called *chidee*. Spread it on your face for beautiful skin. For a bad facial complexion, take the chidee and mix it with ground sandalwood, almond oil and garbanzo flour to make a paste. This is called *batna*. Massage it into the face until the cheeks are red. It will give you the complexion of a twelve-year-old, even at age fifty! Also beneficial as a facial rub are the inside skins of the cucumber and the papaya.

**For the hands.** Follow these five steps for soft and beautiful hands: 1. Rub your hands vigorously with milk for several minutes. 2. Wash your hands with warm water mixed with lemon juice. 3. Wash your hands in warm water. 4. Soak your hands in a milk bath for several minutes. 5. Rinse them with clear water. As an alternative, massage your hands well with almond oil before bed. Wrap them loosely with cotton cloth, and put on gloves. In the morning, wash hands with water but no soap. In a few days, your hands will show the difference.

**Internal skin care.** Chamomile tea, green grapes and papayas will help to give you a clear complexion. Lecithin, taken as a liquid, helps to balance out the oils in the body which may help with bad skin conditions. Fasting on boiled wheatberries one day a week cleans the intestinal tract and helps to make the skin beautiful. Turmeric is good for the skin as is sarsaparilla. A mono diet of green vegetables or steamed zucchinis with additional chlorophyll supplements may help a bad complexion. *Also see Old-Fashioned Root Beer and Yogi Mush.*

**Dry scaling skin,** in the ear for example, may be an indication that the body is deficient in phosphorus or other nerve-building elements. Good sources of phosphorus are: bananas, coconuts and olives.

**For eczema and warts,** the milky juice of the papaya has been drunk for centuries. *Also see Old-Fashioned Root Beer.*

**For burns.** A paste of raw ground potatoes can be applied to superficial burns due to fire.

## SPLEEN
The most common causes of spleen problems are bad water, alcohol, too much hot food, and not drinking enough water when thirsty.

To care for the spleen, the following diets are recommended: 1. Once every six months for ten days, eat only light food such as well-cooked vegetable soup or well-steamed vegetables. Drink lots of water, water with lemon and honey, and light juices such as peach juice or plum juice. Avoid all fats and oils. 2. For ten days, eat only ripe fruit. Once a day, have a salty drink such as grapefruit juice with salt, or simply water with salt. (This diet is not suitable for persons with high blood pressure.) 3. Fast for one week on homemade, unrefrigerated yogurt and water.

Olives are also healthful to the spleen.


## STOMACH

To stimulate stomach acids and aid digestion, the following foods may be helpful. Chiles stimulate the flow of enzymes and hydrochloric acid in the stomach. Citrus, taken an hour or less before meals, activates stomach acids. Drinking lots of water also helps increase hydrochloric acid. Sleeping on the stomach will increase the flow of gastric juices.

Other foods which aid in digestion include apples eaten at the end of a meal, onions, carrots, papaya, and sarsaparilla. *See Old-Fashioned Root Beer and Beet-Carrot Casserole.*

For bloating, drink 12 ounces of cucumber juice per day.

For ulcers, the milky juice of the papaya has been known to help.

For vomiting. Sometimes you have a condition where you vomit little by little without stop. In this case, 1/2 cup of mint tea mixed with 1/2 cup of onion juice may help. If you cannot take that, then take 1/2 cup of cool mint tea mixed with 1/2 cup of a cola soft drink.

For stomach irritation, eat apples stewed in water with lemon peels, honey and a little cinnamon.

**For gas in the bottom of the stomach,** sprinkle ground black pepper on your food.

**To cleanse the stomach and intestines,** saute orange peels in olive oil with a little turmeric. (Be sure to clean the orange peels first to remove wax.) Add water and cover for 5 minutes. Caution: this dish is very laxative.

## UNDERWEIGHT
Losing weight is difficult. Gaining weight, for most people, is easy. However, for those who are chronically underweight, the following foods, included regularly in the diet, may be helpful: bananas, beets, almonds, coconuts and mangoes. *Also see Split Milk Shake and Weight-Gain Pie.*

## URINARY SYSTEM
**For urinary problems,** a beet-greens fast is sometimes effective. Also helpful in urinary disorders are coconut and melons.

**To cleanse the urinary tract,** drink a mixture of 2 parts spinach juice and 1 part carrot juice. Drink a minimum of 1 quart per day.

**To increase urination,** try grapefruit juice. It is a natural diuretic. Pineapple juice also stimulates urination because of its high chlorine content.

**To cleanse the kidneys,** twice a day drink 1 cup of milk with 4 cups of water and some honey. The best time to cleanse the kidneys is during the full moon.

**To stimulate the kidneys** in order to eliminate wastes, the following foods are effective: pineapple, watercress, coconut, rice, and curry on rice. *(See Yogurt Curry.)* A 28-day diet of *Mung Beans and Rice* is also beneficial to the kidneys.

# Recipes

## ANTI-SMOG PANCAKES

When you're feeling tired and dragged out on account of air pollution, these spicy pancakes will pick you up.

*2 1/3 cups garbanzo flour*
*1/3 Tbsp. clove powder*
*1/3 Tbsp. cinnamon powder*
*1/3 Tbsp. cardamon powder*
*1/4 Tbsp. ground black pepper*
*2/3 Tbsp. fennel seeds*
*1/2 Tbsp. caraway seeds*
*1/2 Tbsp. crushed mint leaves*
*1/3-1 1/2 Tbsp. crushed red chiles (some like it hot!)*
*1/2 Tbsp. salt*
*1/3 Tbsp. black salt*
*2/3 Tbsp. parsley flakes*
*2/3 Tbsp. sweet basil*
*1/3 Tbsp. turmeric*
*2/3 Tbsp. cumin powder*
*1/2 medium onion, chopped*
*3 large cloves garlic, chopped*
*1/3 Tbsp. finely chopped ginger root*
*1-2 Jalapeno chiles, chopped*

Blend onion, garlic, ginger and jalapenos with 1 cup water. Mix other ingredients with about 6 cups water to make a thickish batter. Stir in jalapeno mixture. Fry in butter or ghee and cook like pancakes. Serve with yogurt.
Yields 25-30 small pancakes.

# BANANA-NUTMEG ICECREAM

Nutmeg, taken alone, is a very intoxicating food. It can make you totally disoriented. Dried powdered nutmeg can cause severe dizziness and should not be eaten except in minute quantities. Fresh whole nutmeg taken with banana, however, is a tonic, especially for men. It can keep a normal person young for a long time. This recipe can be served as a hot drink or as icecream.

*1 cup milk*
*3 medium-size ripe bananas*
*1 whole nutmeg, ground*
*1 fresh apple, peeled and cored*
*1/3-1/2 cup honey*

Grind nutmeg with mortar and pestle or using a Molinex grinder. Blend ingredients until smooth. Then serve hot or pour into icecream maker and churn until ready.

Makes 1 pt.

To make "icecream" without an icecream maker, pour mixture into a flat tray. Set in freezer until almost frozen solid. Puree in blender. Then freeze again. Puree a second time. Freeze once more and serve.

# BEET-CARROT CASSEROLE

This dish is cleansing to the liver and the digestive tract. To help your body do its own inner cleaning, eat as a mono diet for one week in the spring or fall.

| | |
|---|---|
| *2 bunches scallions, chopped* | *1 lb. carrots* |
| *3 cloves garlic, minced* | *soy sauce* |
| *ghee or vegetable oil* | *ground black pepper* |
| *1 bunch beets* | *1 lb. grated cheese* |

Scrub beets and carrots. Steam beets whole. (Don't cut off roots or stems.) After about 15-20 minutes, add carrots. Steam until tender but firm. Then remove outer peels from beets and carrots. (These should easily slip off.) Grate using a coarse grater. Keep beets and carrots separate to preserve their distinct colors. Saute scallions and garlic in oil or ghee until tender. Toss with beets and carrots and black pepper. Place in casserole dish. Sprinkle with tamari. Cover with grated cheese and broil until cheese is melted and golden.

Serves 4-6.

## CELERY PANCAKES

Pancakes made with celery may sound strange, but wait until you taste them! They will purify your blood and strengthen your central nervous system.

*1/2 tsp. caraway seeds*
*1/2 tsp. oregano seeds*
*1/2 tsp. cumin seeds*
*1/2 tsp. fresh ground black pepper*
*1/2 tsp. celery seeds*
*1 cup finely chopped celery*
*1 cup garbanzo flour*
*1/2 tsp. salt*
*ghee*

Mix ingredients in a bowl, adding water to form a smooth pancake batter. Fry in ghee like a pancake. Serve with yogurt or sourcream.

Makes 8-10 pancakes.

# CHILES AND CHEESE

*8 large Anaheim chiles*
*1/4 - 1/2 cup unprocessed cheese*
*1/2 cup onions, chopped*
*1/4 cup olives, chopped*
*1/4 cup mushrooms, chopped*
*8 tsp. sourcream*
*1 cup basmati rice*
*1 tsp. cumin powder*
*olive oil*

Rinse rice well. Bring to a boil in 3 cups of water, then simmer for 20 minutes until light and puffy. Spoon rice into a lightly oiled casserole dish. Sprinkle with olive oil and cumin powder.

Remove skins from chiles as follows: Toast chiles by holding them over an open gas flame, or by broiling them in the oven on a cookie sheet. When the skins have become charred, wrap the chiles in a cold, wet towel so that the skins "steam off." Then, as you slide the chiles out of their skins, hold them over the bed of cooked rice so that the flavorful chile juice soaks into the rice.

Slice chiles in half, and set them on top of the rice. Stuff chiles with chopped onions, olives and mushrooms. Slice cheese into thin strips about the same length and width as the chiles and set on top of the stuffing. Top chiles with sour cream. Bake at 350 degrees until cheese is melted and serve.

Serves 4.

# COCONUT ICECREAM

Here's a delicious treat that will help to balance the minerals in your body. It's especially recommended for children.

*1 Tbsp. coconut oil*
*1/2 cup coconut meat*
*1 Tbsp. peanut oil*
*1 cup milk*
*3 ripe bananas*
*1/4 tsp. ground cardamon seeds*
*1/8 tsp. powdered cloves*
*1/2 cup honey*

Grind coconut in a Molinex grinder or food processor. Boil milk until a thick skin has formed on the top. Place all ingredients in blender, being sure to include the white strings of the bananas which cling to the peels. Blend to an even consistency. Place in an icecream maker with ice and rock salt and churn until thick and creamy. If you don't have an icecream maker, see recipe for Banana-Nutmeg Icecream to learn how to make icecream without one.
Serves 3-4.

# DATEMILK

This is a very nourishing, youth maintaining beverage. It gives energy to the body and is good for people of all ages, especially when they are recovering from fevers or other diseases.

*8 oz. milk*
*6 dates*

Slice dates in half. Simmer in milk on a very low heat for 20 minutes, stirring occasionally. Strain and serve.

# DRIED HONEY APPLES

This is a "poor man's food" for a healthy heart.

*1 or more apples or carrots*
*honey*
*glass jar*
*cheesecloth*

Steam an apple (or carrot) and peel off the skin. Soak it in honey in a glass jar, cover the jar with cheesecloth, and leave it in the sun for 40 days (cloudy days don't count.) At the end of that time, all the moisture will have gone out of the apple, and the honey will have gone in. Remove from honey and eat. Can also be served with gold leaf or silver leaf.

# EGGPLANT PAKORAS

Eggplant is the "sexiest" food for women. These tasty pakoras make a delicious meal and will help to regulate a woman's menstrual flow.

| | |
|---|---|
| *1 eggplant* | *2 tsp. salt* |
| *2 cups garbanzo flour* | *1 tsp. black pepper* |
| *1 Tbsp. caraway seeds* | *1/2 tsp. ground cloves* |
| *1 tsp. oregano seeds* | *1/2 cup milk* |
| *1 tsp. cardamon seeds* | *3/4 cup onion juice or puree* |
| *1/2 tsp. cinnamon* | *1/3 cup water* |
| *2 tsp. turmeric* | *1/4 cup honey* |

Slice eggplant about 3/8 of an inch thick and set aside. Mix seeds and spices with the garbanzo flour. Add onion juice and milk and stir into smooth paste. Mix with fork until there are no lumps. Dip the eggplant slices in the batter and fry in vegetable oil or ghee until they are golden brown. Set on a paper towel to drain and then serve with catsup or chutney.

Serves 4-6.

# FRUIT BRAN BREAD

3/4 cup wheat bran
1 1/2 cup whole wheat flour
1/2 tsp. salt
1 tsp. baking soda
1 tsp. baking powder

1/3 cup melted ghee
1/2 cup milk
1/2 cup honey
1 cup fresh diced fruit

Sift together dry ingredients. Mix well. Add all other ingredients and stir until well blended. Pour into a greased loaf pan. Bake at 350 degrees for 1 hour. When bread has cooled, remove from pan and slice.

# GARLIC TOAST

Here is a tasty way to eat your "two cloves of garlic a day." Makes a great breakfast food.

2 slices whole grain bread
2-4 medium cloves garlic
ghee

Peel and thinly slice garlic. Lightly toast bread in toaster. Spread liberally with ghee. Top with garlic slices. Place in broiler or toaster oven for no more than 5 minutes. Serve. For variety, top with a thin slice of cheese before broiling.

# GHEE

To make ghee, simmer sweet butter for 10 minutes over a medium heat. Regular salted butter can be used if sweet butter isn't available but it is not as good. Then after it has set for a few minutes remove all the white foam from the top. Clear yellow ghee will be left. Pour this into a container, not allowing any white sediment at the bottom of the pan to slide in. Use as you would butter or cooking oil.

## GOLDEN FIGS

A great potency food for men, but good for women as well. Eat no more than three per day, morning, afternoon and evening.

*10-15 perfect fresh figs*
*1/2 cup milk*
*1 Tbsp. saffron*
*1 clean syringe (available at many pharmacies without the needle.)*

Soak saffron overnight in milk. In the morning, blend milk and saffron until smooth. Carefully wash figs. Draw milk and saffron into syringe and inject the "nectar" into the figs. Make as many as you like and store in the freezer.

## GOLDEN FIG-NUT CHUTNEY

This healthful and delicious chutney (or jam) is great for men and women alike. For a wonderfully balanced and healthful meal, serve with *Eggplant Pakoras* and a perfectly ripe banana (for potassium).

*20 peeled almonds*
*20 raw unsalted pistachio nuts*
*10 Golden Figs (see recipe above)*
*3-4 thin slices ginger root (optional)*

Prepare Golden Figs at least one day before. Place ingredients in blender, add 1/4 cup water, and blend to make a smooth jam. Yields approx. 1 cup.

# GOLDEN MILK

This delicious hot drink is very good for the spine. It lubricates all the joints and helps to break up calcium deposits.

*1/8 tsp. turmeric*
*1/4 cup water*
*8 oz. milk*
*2 Tbsp. raw almond oil*
*honey to taste*

Boil turmeric in water for about 8 minutes until it forms a thick paste. If too much water boils away, add a little more water. Meanwhile, bring milk to a boil with the almond oil. As soon as it boils, remove from heat. Combine the two mixtures and add honey to taste.

If you like, you can prepare a "reserve supply" of turmeric paste by boiling a larger quantity of turmeric and storing in the refrigerator up to 40 days.

As a change of pace, whiz golden milk in the blender until frothy, and serve with a sprinkle of cinnamon.

# HOMEMADE YOGURT

*1 qt. milk*
*2-3 Tbsp. yogurt*

Place milk in a saucepan. Heat it slowly so as not to scorch it. Just short of boiling, remove it from the heat and let cool to a lukewarm temperature, about 118 degrees F. As it cools, stir it occasionally. Then add 2-3 Tbsp. of already made yogurt as a "starter" and stir gently and thoroughly. You can leave the milk in the saucepan, covered, or can pour it into a sterilized jar with a lid. Wrap tightly in a towel to hold in the heat, and place in a warm, dark place where the temperature can be maintained for 6-7 hours. A gas oven with only the pilot light on works well. An insulated cooler, or even a cardboard carton covered with a blanket will usually do the trick. Let it sit undisturbed. The temperature must be neither too hot nor too cold, or the yogurt will not form. After 6-7 hours, you may remove it from its "hiding place" and refrigerate. To grow a stronger yogurt culture (for more acidophilus in your yogurt), allow to sit out at room temperature for from three hours to three days.

## JALAPENO MILK

This is a great drink for heading off a cold or flu when you feel one coming on. But be careful! It's hot. If you've never tried it before, use only the minimum quantity of jalapenos. One more piece of advice — it's not quite so hot if you drink it with a straw.

*2-5 fresh jalapeno chiles*
*8 oz. milk*

Chop jalapenos and blend with milk.

## MANGO LASSI

Here is a cooling and refreshing beverage which is an excellent food for both women and men.

*2 cups homemade yogurt*
*2 medium mangoes (very ripe)*
*3 Tbsp. maple syrup or honey*
*6 ice cubes*
*1/8 tsp. rose water*

Peel and slice mangoes. Put all ingedients in the blender and blend at high speed. Serves 4-6.

## "MS. WHIZ"
Here's a perfect breakfast drink for women. A woman can use this drink to take her daily dose of sesame oil or almond oil. (*See Chapter Seven.*) To lose weight, use 2 Tbsp. protein powder in place of the cold-pressed oil and drink four times per day instead of meals.

*1 ripe banana*
*8 oz. orange juice*
*1 Tbsp. liquid chlorophyl*
*2 tsp. Rice Bran Syrup*
*2 tsp. cold-pressed almond oil or sesame oil*

Blend until frothy.

## MUNG BEANS AND RICE
This is a perfect pre-digested food. It is easy on the digestive system and very nourishing.

*1 cup mung beans*
*1 cup basmati rice*
*9 cups water*
*4-6 cups chopped assorted vegetables (carrots, celery,*
*    zucchini, broccoli, etc.)*
*2 onions, chopped*
*1/3 cup minced ginger root*          *1 tsp. crushed red chiles*
*8-10 cloves garlic, minced*          *1 Tbsp. sweet basil*
*1 heaping tsp. turmeric*             *2 bay leaves*
*1/2 tsp. pepper*                     *seeds of 5 cardamon pods*
*1 heaping tsp. garam masala*         *salt or soy sauce to taste*

Rinse beans and rice. Bring water to a boil, add rice and beans and let boil over a medium flame. Prepare vegetables. Add vegetables to cooking rice and beans. Heat about 1/2 cup oil in large frying pan. Add onions, garlic and ginger and saute over a medium-high flame until browning. Add spices (not salt or herbs). When nicely done, combine onions with cooking mung beans and rice. You will need to stir the dish often to prevent scorching. Add herbs. Continue to cook until completely well done over a medium-low flame, stirring often. The consistency should be rich, thick and soup-like, with ingredients barely discernible. Serve with yogurt, or with cheese melted over the top.

Serves 4-6.

# NUT CURRY SUPREME

This is an almost perfect food for women. Almonds are for the eyes, watermelon seeds for anemia, walnuts for the brain, and chiles for the intestinal tract. It can be served plain, with rice, with chapatis or with pakoras.

*1 large raw onion, chopped*
*4 cloves garlic, finely chopped*
*1 1/2 inches fresh peeled ginger root, finely chopped*
*1-2 green chiles, chopped*
*1/4 cup ghee*
*3 rounded Tbsp. garbanzo flour*
*1/4 cup lemon juice*
*2 tsp. turmeric*
*1 1/2 tsp. cumin*
*1 1/2 tsp. coriander*
*1 1/2 tsp. garam masala*
*4 cups yogurt or buttermilk*
*1/8 cup peeled almonds*
*1/8 cup walnuts*
*1/4 cup cashews, pecans or apricot kernels*
*1/8 cup watermelon or pumpkin seeds*
*2 zucchinis, chopped*

Mix 1/4 cup yogurt or buttermilk with garbanzo flour and stir until it forms a smooth paste. Then stir into the rest of the yogurt or buttermilk.

Saute onions in ghee until they are clear to golden brown. Add chiles, ginger and garlic and saute until ginger and garlic are golden. Add turmeric and saute on a low heat until golden brown. Then add other spices. Add yogurt or buttermilk mixture. Then add lemon juice. Continue cooking on low heat. Add zucchinis, nuts and seeds and continue simmering until zucchinis are soft.

Serves 4.

## OLD-FASHIONED ROOT BEER

For a delicious cooling drink, try this "old-fashioned" recipe. Sarsaparilla is a great blood purifier. It is said to be helpful in cases of rheumatism, skin disorders, sexual impotence, general weakness, and to detoxify the body after taking a strong poison. (Do not attempt to use as an antidote.) It is also used as a natural stimulant of the male and female sex hormones.

*7 cups honey*
*2 oz. sarsaparilla extract*
*4 1/2 cups hot water*
*sparkling water*

To make the syrup, dissolve honey and sarsparilla in hot water and stir until thoroughly blended. Add 2 Tbsp. of this syrup to sparkling water and drink.

## PANEER

*1/2 gallon milk*
*juice of 2 lemons*

Put milk in saucepan and bring to boil. Add juice of 1 lemon for each quart of milk. Stir and allow to boil another few seconds. When curdled, strain through cheesecloth and squeeze liquid out to achieve desired consistency. For vegetable dishes like saag it should be very dry.

# PARSLEY PILAU

This is a very good male food. (Women enjoy it also.) It is useful when you get headaches or feel a heaviness in your head, or when you feel unnecessarily sleepy. It is very good for the brain and can be eaten as a mono diet. For extra energy, if you must work very hard, eat with yogurt.

*1 cup basmati rice*
*1 cup parsley*
*2 cups unskinned chopped potatoes*
*2 onions*
*2 tsp. oregano seeds*
*1 tsp. ground red pepper (or add more to taste)*
*1 Tbsp. turmeric*
*1 tsp. black pepper*
*2 crushed bay leaves*
*1/2 cup ghee*

Saute onions in ghee. Add spices and cook until browned. Then add rice, potatoes and parsley and stir for a while. Add water (to steam the rice), cover, and cook for another 15 minutes. Serves 4-6.

# PISTACHIO PARANTHAS

This food is known as a natural remedy for arthritis. Used as such, it can be taken as a mono diet. It can also help a man to build his potency, or to repair damage to his sexual organs. For this purpose, a man should one day a week eat two paranthas and nothing else.

Flour:
*1/2 cup corn flour*
*1/2 cup garbanzo flour*
*1/2 cup bhajara flour (if not available, use whole wheat flour)*
*3 cups whole wheat flour*

Stuffing:
1 lb. pistachio nuts - raw, shelled, unsalted

| | |
|---|---|
| 1 cup minced cauliflower | 2 tsp. salt |
| 1 chopped onion | 1 tsp. pepper |
| 2 tsp. saffron | 1/4 cup milk |
| 1 tsp. ground red chiles | ghee |

Soak saffron overnight in milk. In morning, blend until smooth. Finely chop stuffing ingredients and mix well, or blend in food processor to form a fine mixture. Mix the flours with water to form a doughy consistency.

Knead the dough for a while, then place a golf ball size ball on a floured surface and roll to about a 6 inch diameter. Place about 1/2 cup of the stuffing in the middle, then bring up the sides of the dough around it, pinching it together at the top to seal the stuffing inside. Roll it out again into a flattened 6 inch diameter. Cook for 10-15 minutes over a low flame on a dry chapati pan or frying pan. Then turn it over and pour melted ghee on top of the parantha. It will seep through to the other side. Cook for about 5 minutes, pressing the top of the parantha with a spoon until thoroughly cooked. Serve with yogurt.

Makes about 12 medium paranthas.

## POTENCY POTION
A great men's breakfast drink to overcome impotency:

1 cup milk
6 peeled almonds
seeds from 3 cardamon pods, crushed
1/2 tsp. honey

Blend until frothy. For best results, do not eat again for 4 hours.

# POTENT POTATOES

4 russet baking potatoes
1/2 cup oil
3 onions, chopped
1/4 cup ginger, minced
1 bulb garlic, minced
1 tsp. black pepper
1 1/2 tsp. turmeric
1 tsp. crushed red chiles or cayenne
8 whole cloves
seeds of 3 cardamon pods
1/2 tsp. ground cinnamon
1/3 cup soy sauce
1/2 pint cattage cheese
4 slices cheese, cut in half
1 bell pepper, finely diced
1/2 cup pineapple, chopped and drained


Bake potatoes for about 1 hour, until nice and soft on the inside and crispy on the outside. Meanwhile, heat oil in skillet and add onions and ginger. Saute until onions are well done, then add garlic and spices. If spices are sticking to the pan, add more oil. Cook until browned. Add soy sauce. Cut baked potatoes in half lengthwise. Scoop out the insides and combine with the onion mixture. Add cottage cheese. Refill potato shells forming mounds on top. Cover with slices of cheese and broil until melted and golden. Garnish with bell peppers and pineappple.
Serves 4-8.

# SAFFRON ALMOND RICE
This is a recipe to enhance a man's creativity.

| | |
|---|---|
| 1 cup milk | 1/2 tsp. cinnamon |
| 1 tsp. saffron | 1 tsp. salt |
| 1 1/2 cups basmati rice | 1/2 cup almonds |
| 6 cloves garlic | 1 Tbsp. ghee |
| 2 cups homemade yogurt | |

To guard against viral infections, add the following seeds:
1/6 cup watermelon seeds
1/6 cup zucchini seeds
1/6 cup pumpkin seeds


Soak saffron in milk overnight. In morning, blend until smooth. Soak almonds overnight or in boiling water to remove the skins. Then slice almonds. Peel and slice garlic cloves in quarters. Saute garlic and almonds in ghee. Rinse rice thoroughly. Boil basmati rice in saffron milk and 2 cups water. Add garlic and almonds. Simmer for 20 minutes. Serve with yogurt. (Add saffron milk when dish is half-cooked.)

If there is a need to cleanse the internal organs, then eat this dish with "Golden Yogurt." Boil 1/2 tsp. turmeric in 1 qt. milk. Use this milk to make yogurt.

Serves 4-6.


# SAAG PANEER

| | |
|---|---|
| 5 bunches mustard greens | 1 tsp. salt |
| 2 large onions, finely chopped | 1/2 tsp. crushed red chiles |
| 2 tsp. turmeric | 5 ripe tomatoes, peeled |
| 2 Tbsp. cumin | 1/2 cup ghee |
| 2 Tbsp. coriander | 1/4 tsp. black pepper |

120

At least 3-4 hours in advance, make *paneer (see recipe)*. Wrap paneer in cheesecloth and hang over sink to drain until all the liquid has come out.

Rinse mustard greens thoroughly, then coarsely chop. Set to boil for at least 2 hours. Check the water periodically to avoid scorching. Place in blender and blend until smooth. Then pour into a large saucepan and continue to cook over a medium flame.

While the mustard greens are boiling, remove paneer from cheesecloth and set on a board. Kneed it as you would bread until it is smooth and soft. Roll it out with a rolling pin to a thickness of 1 inch. Then use your hands to shape the paneer into a 1 inch thick rectangle. Cut paneer into 1 inch cubes. Heat ghee or oil in a frypan and deep fry paneer until golden brown. Set aside.

Saute onions in ghee or oil over a medium-high heat until brown. Add spices and saute a few minutes longer. Then add tomatoes and crushed chiles and cook until saucy. Add to cooked greens with 1/4 cup ghee and cook until the extra water has cooked out and the saag is thick. Add in paneer. Salt to taste. Serves 4-6.

## SESAME-GINGER MILK

This creamy and stimulating drink is nourishing to the nervous system and to the male sexual organs. Tasty too!

*1/4 cup sesame seeds*
*2 Tbsp. coarsely chopped ginger root (very fresh)*
*12 oz. milk*
*2 tsp. honey or maple syrup*

Blend at high speed until smooth and frothy. Makes about 2 cups.

# SESAME SOURDOUGH BREAD

| | |
|---|---|
| *1 package sourdough starter* | *1 package dry yeast* |
| *4 cups sesame seeds* | *2 tsp. salt* |
| *1 oz. sesame oil* | *1 1/2 cup warm milk* |
| *5 cups whole wheat flour* | *3 cups chopped peeled apples* |
| *2 Tbsp. honey* | *2 Tbsp. melted butter* |

Prepare sourdough starter as per package directions. (You'll need to do this about four days in advance.) Blend sesame seeds with sesame oil to make sesame butter. Set aside. Put 3 cups sourdough starter in a warm bowl. Stir in (in order) 1 cup whole wheat flour, honey, dry yeast, salt, warm milk, 2 cups sesame butter, chopped apples and melted butter. Stir well. Stir in 4 more cups whole wheat flour.

Knead bread on a well-floured board until smooth and elastic. Lightly oil the dough and place in a large warm bowl. Allow to rise for about 2 hrs. until double size. Punch down and let rise again for 30 minutes. Divide dough into two equal loaves. Place in well-greased loaf pans. (Dough should fill the pans no more than half full.) Allow to rise for about 90 minutes. Oil the top of each loaf. Bake in pre-heated oven at 375 degrees for 45 minutes. Remove from loaf pans. For a softer crust, oil or butter sides and bottom immediately.

# SESAME YOGURT DRESSING

This is a perfectly balanced salad dressing for women. (Don't tell that to the men and they'll enjoy it too.)

*4 sprigs parsley*
*1 stalk celery, chopped*
*1/2 cup sesame seeds*
*1/4 small onion, chopped*
*1 clove garlic, sliced*
*1/2 cup raw sesame oil*

*1 Tbsp. vinegar*
*2 Tbsp. lemon juice*
*1/2 tsp. salt*
*1/4 tsp. ground black pepper*
*1 tsp. honey*
*2 Tbsp. soy sauce*
*1 cup yogurt*

Blend until smooth and serve.
Makes about 3 cups.

## SOLSTICE HOT SAUCE

Each year, the 3HO "family" holds its "Summer Solstice Sadhana" in Espanola, New Mexico. It is a chance for people to purify their minds, souls and bodies through practicing lots of Kundalini and Tantric Yoga, eating very cleansing food, drinking the purest water, and breathing clean air. As part of the healing diet, this special hot sauce made with native New Mexican chiles is always served.

*3 large onions, chopped*
*1/4 cup dry crushed red chiles*
*8 oz. tamarind concentrate*
*16 oz. hot water*
*1 1/2 cup sesame oil*
*1 Tbsp. turmeric*
*10 whole small dry red chiles*
*2 cups apple cider vinegar*

Put onions in a large bowl. Sprinkle with crushed chiles. Melt tamarind concentrate in hot water. Add oil and diluted tamarind to onions. Sprinkle with turmeric. Add whole chiles and vinegar. Stir and cover. Let sit overnight or several days for the fullest flavor. Store in refrigerator. It will keep a long time, and get better and better. Yields 2 quarts.

# SPICED CHAPATIS

In India, when someone gets a fever, they make him one of these special chapatis (flat breads). It makes a person sweat, and the fever comes down.

*2 cups whole wheat flour*
*ghee*
*1 tsp. black pepper*
*1/2 tsp. cinnamon*
*1/2 tsp. cardamon*
*1 tsp. fennel seeds*

Place flour in bowl. Mix in spices. Stir in enough water to make a soft dough that comes away from the sides of the bowl. Add more flour if necessary. Knead the dough until it is smooth, soft and springy, and not at all sticky. Heat an iron skillet over a medium-high heat. Form dough into ping-pong size balls. Then flatten into squat patties. Flour patties on both sides and roll out on a lightly floured board into 6 inch diameter circles, not more than 1/8 inch thick.

Place on hot skillet. Cook on the first side until lightly crusted — not even browned. Flip over and cook second side the same way. Either place the chapati directly over a gas flame, flipping it once or twice so that it puffs up, or flip it over in the pan and lightly press on it with a spatula or paper towel to make it puff up. Then, flip it over again and do the same thing on the other side. When properly done, there should be only a sprinkling of brown spots on either side. If the chapati browns rapidly the heat is too high.

As each one is done, spread butter or melted ghee on top of it and stack. (The the top of one chapati will butter the bottom of the next.)

Yields 8-12 chapatis.

# SPLIT MILK SHAKE

Here is a great protein drink which you can substitute for a meal, or add to your meals for gaining weight. For quick weight gain, drink one glass four times a day.

*8 oz. milk*
*juice of 1/2 lemon*
*4 ripe bananas*
*4 Tbsp. Rice Bran Syrup*
*4 Tbsp. quality protein powder*
*2 oz. chlorophyll*

Bring milk to a boil, then remove from heat. Add lemon juice and stir. The milk should "split," that is separate into curds and whey. Allow to cool, then pour split milk into the blender, add additional ingredients, and blend at medium speed.

# TRINITY RICE

A real treat! This dish is said to be especially good for people who are sick or suffering from blood poisoning.

*2 onions, chopped*
*2 cloves garlic, peeled and sliced*
*1 inch ginger root, peeled and grated*
*1 cup basmati rice*
*1/2-3/4 cup ghee*
*1 tomato, peeled*
*4-5 cups assorted chopped vegetables*

Rinse basmati rice thoroughly. Saute spices in ghee until golden brown. Add onion, garlic and ginger ("trinity roots") and stir slowly until onions begin falling apart. Then add tomato, assorted vegetables and rice, along with 4 cups of water. Cover and let simmer on a low heat, checking frequently. Add water as necessary. Cook until vegetables are soft and rice is done. Serves 4.

## TRINITY SAFFRON NUT SPREAD

This food is said to give a man endurance, strengthen his nerves and enrich his semen. Spread on bread or crackers. Eat no more than once a week, and be sure to have it with milk.

1 large onion
3 cloves garlic
2 inches peeled ginger root
50 raw unsalted pistachios, shelled

40 peeled almonds
15 strands dried saffron
1/2 cup milk
1/4-1/3 cup honey

Soak pistachios, almonds and saffron overnight in milk. Chop and steam onions, garlic and ginger until soft. Blend with saffron nut milk, adding honey and a little water. Blend thoroughly until it forms a smooth paste. Yields about 12 oz.


## WEIGHT-GAIN PIE

This unique beet-apple pie is a favorite for any meal, and a sure way to put on weight.

5 medium beets
5 apples, peeled and thin-sliced
2 cups cottage cheese
4 Tbsp. ghee
1/2 cup almonds, peeled and chopped
2 Tbsp. finely chopped ginger
1/4 tsp. ground cinnamon
1 1/2 cups whole wheat flour
1 stick butter
3/4 tsp. salt

Lightly steam beets and allow to cool. Rinse under cold water to slip off outer skins.

Mix salt and flour. Chop butter into flour and add in ice cold water, mixing until flour is stiff. Roll out and shape into lightly oiled pie pan.

Lightly saute ginger and cinnamon in ghee. Stir in sliced apples and simmer for 10 minutes.

Layer beets and apples in pie shell. Cover with cottage cheese and sprinkle with chopped almonds. Bake at 350 degrees for 45 minutes. Allow 10 minutes to cool before serving.

Serves 4.


# WEIGHT-LOSS TEA
### (Jaalaa Jeeraa)

This tea has be used by men or women to dissolve fatty tissue from their bodies. For this purpose, drink 2-3 glasses per day. It also improves the beauty of the skin, giving a youthful appearance. For the skin, drink 2 glasses per day. It cleanses the mucous membrane of the colon and is an excellent source of Vitamin C.

*1/2-3/4 cup fresh or dried mint leaves*
*1 lb. cumin seeds*
*1 oz. fresh or frozen tamarind*
*1/2 tsp. black salt (also called sulfur salt. Use only a little. It has a strong smell.)*
*8 lemons, quartered.*
*1 Tbsp. black pepper*
*5 qts. water*

Put ingredients in a pot. Bring to a boil. Lower the flame and cook at a low boil for 4-5 hours. This much time is required to draw the extract from the cumin seeds. Strain and serve hot or cold. You can re-use the ingredients to make more tea. Just add a little more each time you boil. Be sure to remove the lemon peels between boilings. Tea can be stored up to a week in the refrigerator.

# YOGI MUSH

This food, when eaten regularly, will cleanse the intestines, clear the skin, and help you lose weight. When taken as a mono diet, eat as much as you like, but only three meals per day. You can drink yogi tea with this diet.

| | |
|---|---|
| *4 celery stalks* | *1 sprig mint* |
| *1 bunch parsley* | *1/2 tsp. ground black pepper* |
| *4-5 medium zucchinis* | *1 cup cottage cheese* |

Steam celery, parsley, zucchinis and mint for about 15 minutes until soft. Puree with black pepper. Serve with cottage cheese. Makes about 2 servings.


# YOGI TEA

Make at least 4 cups of Yogi Tea at a time. (One is never enough!) For each cup, use:

*10 oz. water*
*3 cloves*
*4 green cardamon pods*
*4 whole black peppers*
*1/2 stick cinnamon*
*1 slice ginger root*
*1/4 tsp. black tea*
*1/2 cup milk*

Boil spices for 10-15 minutes. Add black tea and steep for 2 minutes. Add milk, then reheat to the boiling point, remove immediately from the stove, and strain. Add honey to taste.

To make more than 1 qt., you can use less spices. For 2 qts., use 20 cardamon pods, 20 peppercorns, 15 cloves, 3 cinnamon sticks, and 1 tbl. black tea. Boil at least 30 minutes. Add 1 qt. milk.

Spices can be reused to make more tea, but this takes a little experience, since some of the spices lose their potency faster than others and must be replenished. For the beginner, it is best to make a fresh pot every time to insure the proper balance.

*Yogi tea spices are now available pre-mixed, in small packages or in bulk. See Appendix A.*


# YOGURT CURRY

To soothe and strengthen the nervous system, and to please the palate, try this delicious curry.

*1 cup basmati rice*
*3 cups chopped mixed vegetables*
*1/4 cup minced ginger*
*2 cloves garlic, minced*
*2 small onions, finely chopped*
*1/2 cup ghee*
*1 1/2 tsp. crushed yogi tea spices*
*1 Tbsp. turmeric*
*1/4 tsp. oregano seeds*
*1/2 tsp. cumin seeds*
*1/4 tsp. ground black pepper*
*1 tsp. garam masala*
*1 cup homemade yogurt*
*1/4 cup garbanzo flour*

Rinse the rice then add 3 cups water and bring it to a boil. Simmer for about 45 minutes. Steam chopped mixed vegetables until firm but tender. Blend yogurt and garbanzo flour with 1 cup water until smooth. Saute spices in ghee until golden brown. Add chopped onion, garlic and ginger. Cook slowly until onions are almost falling apart. Stir in yogurt-flour mixture. Simmer until sauce thickens. Serve over rice and steamed vegetables. Serves 4.

# Appendix A: Sources for Special Foods

For referrals to local stores, you may use the following options.

- Please contact your local 3HO center by consulting the yellow pages in your telephone directory.

- Some items are available through the Ancient Healing Ways Catalog. For a free catalog:

**Tel 800-359-2940 inside the US**
**Tel 505-747-2860 outside the US**
**Fax 505-747-2868**

# Appendix B: The 3HO Healing Network
## and
## Kundalini Yoga Teaching Centers

There are many health professionals who employ Yogi Bhajan's teachings on health and diet in their healing practices.

The 3HO Foundation has more than one hundred centers worldwide offering Kundalini Yoga, health, and nutrition classes. To find out about the center nearest you, you may use the resources listed below.

For referral information on both of the above, you may contact any of the following:

- IKYTA
  (International Kundalini Yoga Teachers Association)
     Tel: 505-753-0423
     Internet: www.yogi bhajan.com

- The yellow pages telephone directory for the number of your local 3HO center

# Appendix C: Books on Related Topics

**THE GOLDEN TEMPLE VEGETARIAN COOKBOOK**  by Yogi Bhajan. Food to delight and heal your mind, body, and spirit. Many of the recipes are served at internationally famous restaurants.

**TASTE OF INDIA**  by Bibiji Inderjit Kaur. An Indian cookbook for the health conscious gourmet! Here are recipes for the whole person—body, mind, and spirit. These authentic recipes are exotic and yet presented so clearly that they are easy to prepare.

**FROM VEGETABLES WITH LOVE**  by Siri Ved Kaur Khalsa. Vegetarian New World cuisine. Contains over 260 recipes, including 35 recipes from the "community kitchen" devoted to recipes serving 40–100 people.

**SADHANA GUIDELINES**  Kundalini Yoga is the most powerful and effective form of yoga taught today. It is especially suited to the needs of busy people who want to stay calm, bright, and centered in a high energy world. This book contains complete instructions for your daily practice of this ancient science of awareness, as taught by Yogi Bhajan.

*THE MIND : ITS PROJECTIONS AND MULTIPLE FACETS*  by Yogi Bhajan, PhD, and Gurucharan PhD. Yogi Bhajan describes in this book how we can know and understand the Mind so it becomes our ally and not our problem. The Mind is divided into 3 Functional Minds: Neutral, Negative and Positive ~ 9 Aspects; The Defender, The Manager, The Preserver, The Artist, The Producer, The Missionary, The Strategist, The Leader and The Teacher and 27 Projections (there is a Meditations given for each Projection) containing a total of 81 Facets. This book is for everyone that would like to get a deeper understanding of his or her Mind and therefore lead a more happy and fuller life.

*MASTER'S TOUCH*  by Yogi Bhajan. A compilation of Teachings by Yogi Bhajan given during Master's Touch courses in Espanola and Assisi, Italy. The 22 classes given in Espanola cover topics such as "What is Happiness", "Self Reverence", "The Teacher and Student", "Projecting as a Teacher", "The Art of Communication", "The Caliber of a Teacher". The 11 classes of Assisi cover topics such as: "What is Your Reality?", "The Power of the Mind", "Give God a Change" and "Life is a Gift". All these classes will give you a deep and profound understanding of the unique inside of the human character and the Path of The Teacher. The book also includes Yoga Exercises and Meditations.

# INDEX

*138*

*139*

CPSIA information can be obtained at www.ICGtesting.com
Printed in the USA
LVOW08s2044060914

402670LV00007B/6/P